ning done, persuade John Kasich it's a good idea. Debt relief for people on the planet was a crazy notion until he helped explain s later, it was accepted as common sense. Five years later, twice ildren in Uganda were going to school. When he takes something s in, people believe in him. Believe in him.

–BONO

n incredibly important book about the essential moral foundation igion provides for human beings to be able to work together toward n goals. As public servants for many years, John Kasich and I expe- d the awesome force of faith and religion that enabled us to cooperate lve pressing problems in our beloved America.

–DICK GEPHARDT, former Democratic leader, US House of Representatives

John Kasich has written another fantastic book inviting us to find our ultimate meaning in life by giving ourselves to purposes that will outlive us. In his understated yet profound way, John paints a beautiful mosaic of how ordinary people can make extraordinary contributions. He invites us to become others-centered by committing ourselves to the well-being of our communities, and along the way highlights the great contributions being made by several individuals spread across our vast country. Simone Weil once observed that just as the power of the sun is the only power in the natural universe that can get a plant to grow against gravity, so the love of God is the only power in the spiritual universe that can get a human to grow against the power of their egocentrism. John's book is a great invitation to lead a life of loving impact.

–DR. GAYLE D. BEEBE, president, Westmont College

In this book, John Kasich has shined a light on the agency that we all have to be pockets of heaven on earth when we embrace community with one another, love for one another, and service to one another. The stories in this book of faith, forgiveness, hope, love, sacrifice, and service not only are inspiring but also are calls to action for all of us. Communities, particularly our faith communities, are institutions that exist to provide the "people fuel" we get from and give to each other to make our world a better place.

–CLARK KELLOGG, basketball analyst, CBS Sports

John Kasich knows that an individual can make a difference. Su[...]
an individual of faith working within a community of faith can [...]
ger things to change the world for the better. John shares the [...]
ordinary people, like you and me, who, motivated by their faith an[...]
in communities of faith, have brought meaning, joy, and life to the s[...]
and vulnerable. Reading *Heaven Help Us* not only inspired me but m[...]
to want to be like these ordinary people, who turn out to be extraor[...]

—TREMPER LONGMAN III, PhD, distinguished scholar and p[...]
emeritus of biblical studies, Westmon[...]

HEAVEN HELP US

HEAVEN HELP US

How FAITH Communities
Inspire HOPE,
STRENGTHEN Neighborhoods,
and Build THE FUTURE

JOHN KASICH

WITH DANIEL PAISNER

ZONDERVAN
BOOKS

ZONDERVAN BOOKS

Heaven Help Us
Copyright © 2025 by John Kasich

Published in Grand Rapids, Michigan, by Zondervan. Zondervan is a registered trademark of The Zondervan Corporation, L.L.C., a wholly owned subsidiary of HarperCollins Christian Publishing, Inc.

Requests for information should be addressed to customercare@harpercollins.com.

Zondervan titles may be purchased in bulk for educational, business, fundraising, or sales promotional use. For information, please email SpecialMarkets@Zondervan.com.

ISBN 978-0-310-36884-7 (audio)

Library of Congress Cataloging-in-Publication Data

Names: Kasich, John, author. | Paisner, Daniel, author.
Title: Heaven help us : how faith communities inspire hope, strengthen neighborhoods, and build the future / John Kasich with Daniel Paisner.
Description: Grand Rapids, Michigan : Zondervan, [2025]
Identifiers: LCCN 2024056921 (print) | LCCN 2024056922 (ebook) | ISBN 9780310368823 (hardcover) | ISBN 9780310368830 (ebook)
Subjects: LCSH: Religions—Relations. | Social groups—United States. | Communities—Religious aspects—United States. | Dialogue—Religious aspects—United States. | Faith. | BISAC: RELIGION / Religion, Politics & State | RELIGION / Christian Living / Inspirational
Classification: LCC BL410 .K88 2025 (print) | LCC BL410 (ebook) | DDC 206/.50973—dc23/eng/20250103
LC record available at https://lccn.loc.gov/2024056921
LC ebook record available at https://lccn.loc.gov/2024056922

Cover design: Faceout Studio, Spencer Fuller
Cover photo: Shutterstock
Interior design: Denise Froehlich

Printed in the United States of America

25 26 27 28 29 LBC 5 4 3 2 1

*To my wife, Karen,
and my daughters, Emma and Reese.
You are my light and hope.*

CONTENTS

*The first act of love is always
the giving of attention.*

—DALLAS WILLARD

INTRODUCTION

Faith Is Contagious

I published my first book nearly twenty-five years ago—a collection of inspirational profiles of individuals doing good works to bring about meaningful change. *Courage Is Contagious: Ordinary People Doing Extraordinary Things to Change the Face of America* was an immediate *New York Times* bestseller, and one of the messages readers responded to, I think, was the way our subjects were so willing to put the needs of others ahead of their own, and the ways we were able to push each other to reflect on the *essentialness* of their extra efforts.

My hope was that the book would motivate readers to think beyond their own circumstances and get them to share in my excitement and maybe even help them find some inspiration in these stories of people doing amazing things. My focus was on people whom readers had likely never heard of but who were moving mountains nevertheless.

Probably the best example of the relatively anonymous people I celebrated in that book was a man named Albert Lexie, who at the time was living a quiet, unassuming life, working two days a week shining shoes at the Children's Hospital of Pittsburgh. I first heard about Albert through my friend Stu Boehmig, pastor of Pittsburgh's Orchard Hill Church, who reached out to me one day and told me I just had to meet this remarkable man. So I did. And what I found was indeed remarkable. Albert was in the habit back then of donating his tips to the hospital's Free Care Fund, which ensured that all patients receive the medical care they need regardless of their ability to pay.

At the time of our first meeting, Albert was charging just $3 a shine, and yet he had somehow raised more than $40,000 in tips, in just under twenty years. At the time of his death nearly a dozen years later, that number had grown to more than $200,000, and Albert had gained a bit of notoriety in and around town, and even around the country, after word of his generosity spread thanks to appearances on *The Oprah Winfrey Show*, the *CBS Evening News*, and other national programs, and after being honored at the 2010 Major League Baseball All-Star Game and being inducted by the Caring Institute into the Hall of Fame for Caring Americans.

Albert and I kept in touch over the years, up until his death in 2018, and whenever we reconnected, we talked about his powerful example. I am reminded of Albert's quiet heroism in these opening pages for the bridge it offers between that first book and this one right here. For *Courage Is Contagious*, I was out to highlight ordinary people such as Albert who were clearing a path in our society, doing extraordinary things to make our world a better place, in big ways and small. For this book, I'm hoping to grow that concept to include ordinary people doing extraordinary things with the help of their faith-based communities—once again, in big ways and small—because over the years I've come to believe that the good works we do in service of our faith, alongside people who join us in service of that faith, can fundamentally change the world.

Now, it just so happens that Albert Lexie was a man of faith, but he was raising that money on his own and donating it on his own—with no expectation that he would be honored or recognized for his generosity in any way. He was just doing what he thought was right, in what ways he could. And yet his faith couldn't help but shine through. During one of our first visits, he dropped to his knees and started singing "The Old Rugged Cross," a popular hymn from the early 1900s that became a church favorite after it appeared as the title song on Ernest Tubb's 1952 country gospel album.

So I'll cherish the old rugged cross
Till my trophies at last I lay down.
I will cling to the old rugged cross
And exchange it some day for a crown.

My goodness, he sang in such a rich, full voice—it was just awesome. As moving and uplifting as any Springsteen or U2 or Foo Fighters concert I've ever seen. He sang from a place deep in his soul.

I wrote about that moment in *Courage Is Contagious* because it signaled to me the wonderful harmony that often finds us when our good deeds align with our faith. I offer it here as a way to introduce the stories I mean to share in the pages ahead. This time around, I hope not only to inspire readers to live righteously and purposefully in pursuit of making a meaningful difference in the world but also to remind them of the exponential power of faith and our faith-based communities.

The idea for this book started percolating for me during the pandemic, when I got together online with a group of theologians to discuss Christianity. I was helped along in this by my great friend John Palafoutas, one of the founders and leaders of Faith and Law, a community of congressional leaders and staffers that meets regularly to think about how our faith informs our calling to the public square. I was becoming increasingly concerned at what I was hearing about all of these ministers around the country who were under fire from their congregations, with members trying to get them to take a political stand or endorse a particular candidate or issue. They were being knocked off balance because of it. I didn't believe these types of discussions belonged inside the church, so I thought I'd bring together a group of faith leaders to see whether we could come up with a statement these ministers could rely upon—you know, a patch of firm ground on which they all might stand.

I reached out to writers, leaders, and scholars I admired. I won't call out any of them by name here, but I think it's fair to say that my friend John and I somehow assembled a top-tier group of thinkers and theologians to join us on that call.

Well, sometimes what seems like a great notion is not so great after all, because it turned out that we couldn't get these religious thinkers to agree on much. They were all brilliant, make no mistake, but they all had their own ideas—which, looking back, I might have anticipated. It reminded me of my time in Congress, when it was like herding cats trying to get people to come together to pass a balanced budget. It was nearly impossible (which is probably why it hasn't happened since). But trying to get this group to produce a single declarative statement to articulate our shared view of contemporary Christianity was even harder than herding cats, because *these* cats each had their own deeply held convictions, their own agendas. We went round and round and never really got anywhere. In the end we all went our separate ways and retreated back into our separate silos and continued on in our separate lifelong pursuits of religious meaning.

"We need to come together to figure out whether we can work together for the greater good of God and our American society," John and I wrote as a kind of prototype statement to try to get this group on the same page. "This isn't a call to action to engineer a dramatic sea change or a cymbal crash to get us back on course, but simply an invitation to see whether we can agree on the common challenges and on a way forward. We believe we need to practice again the discipline of sitting down with those with whom we agree on some things and disagree on others and discuss again the ideals that have governed and guided our society. This is a conversation that needs to start small, with deliberation and purpose, in such a way that the good news is once again given a chance to spread, one person at a time, one congregation at a time."

As I said, we didn't get very far with these theologians, but the exercise inspired me to start thinking once again about all the amazing people out there with great ideas. Unlike in the run-up to *Courage Is Contagious*, *this* time I was focusing on people who were discovering that our institutions of faith could help them with resources and people. As I did so, I reexamined what it meant to be a person of faith and considered how we might attach that faith to our daily lives—a conversation I continued to have with myself until I thought to grow the idea behind my first book into the framework for this one, to help me celebrate acts of selflessness and generosity and courage, but this time strengthened by the support of a religious community.

I believe a book such as this one has the chance to make the kind of meaningful statement I was hoping to pull from my informal gathering of theologians. I believe, too, that the time is right for this. We are living in perilous times. People are adrift, divided, conflicted—young people especially—and I'm struck by the ways many are stepping away from organized religion. They're put off by the negative headlines or the prevailing notion that our religious leaders are becoming more and more political, or less and less inclusive. I *get* that. To a lot of people, religion is fraught with judgment, rules, and seemingly archaic rituals and practices that might seem out of step with the times. I get that, too. And yet I've come to realize that the ordinary people doing extraordinary things I looked to celebrate in my first book are out there today in even greater force, and that their noble acts of goodwill and community building are being strengthened by the support they're receiving from their religious institutions.

We ought to be paying attention. And we ought to be talking about how we can join them. That's the thing about inspiring stories: They can move us to action. It's not enough to sit back and admire the good works or selfless initiatives of others; they're meant to move us to action and to get us thinking of the ways we might grow our own extra efforts, tapping the many resources to be found in our faith communities.

When I decided to write my first book, I was running for reelection to my ninth term as a member of the US House of Representatives from Ohio's Twelfth Congressional District, and I think the expectation was that because I was a politician I would want to write about politics or policy, or perhaps take the opportunity to share my positions on a variety of social issues. But that sort of thing didn't interest me—I mean, it *did*, because as a public servant these things were at the heart of my life's work, but that was the stuff of my day job. I was spending enough of my time in Washington working to fairly and effectively represent the good people of Ohio and this great nation, but if I was going to roll up my sleeves and set my thoughts to paper in the hope that others might find inspiration between the lines of what I was writing, I wanted to use it as an opportunity to step outside myself and get away from politics and shine some meaningful light on the contributions of others.

Well, I'm still sounding the call for self-reflection and active citizenship, and I'm still firm in my belief in the power of individuals to bring about meaningful change, although I've expanded my thinking on this in the years since I wrote *Courage Is Contagious*. These days, I've come to appreciate how that positive, simple power can be accelerated by our religious institutions in important and compelling ways that will almost always exceed the expectations of the individual who looked to jump-start the initiative in the first place.

When I was governor, my office made it a special point each year to honor ordinary Ohio citizens from all walks of life who were making extraordinary contributions to their communities. These Courage Awards, as we called them, were meant to remind us that good things are possible even in the face of impossible odds, and that it is on each of us to make a meaningful difference in whatever ways we can, and each year I looked forward to the awards ceremony for the chance it offered to reflect on the power of the individual to make a meaningful difference—and to meet some truly wonderful Ohioans.

I continue to be drawn to those stories, and to be inspired by them, but the stories I'm most interested in of late are ones about the difference-makers who are supported in their efforts by their religious communities—you know, the ones that remind us that it's the resourcefulness and ingenuity of our fellow congregants and religious leaders that make it possible for some of us to turn our good intentions into even better outcomes, on an even bigger scale. Why do these stories interest me? In part because they offer not only hope and inspiration but also a map for what we *all* could do. They get us thinking of all the ways our impossible dreams might be made possible.

Here again I find myself looking to motivate readers and to create a kind of blueprint we all might follow, but this time I'm out to highlight the impact that individuals can have when they tap into the elevating authority of our local churches, synagogues, and mosques.

What happens when we realize we can't go it alone? What happens when we realize that we really are better together? What happens when we unlock the generosity, creativity, and grit of not just one person but a whole faith community on the local level? The book you're holding tells what happens. Better, it shows it. And as it shows it, I expect that you'll be inspired and informed to join the cause.

In some ways, *Heaven Help Us* closes the circle on what I set out to do with *Courage Is Contagious* nearly a quarter century ago. Actually, it doesn't close it so much as it opens it up, in a wondrous way—it magnifies the message I shared back when I was in Congress. Once again I'm out to shine a light on the good, courageous work of individuals looking to make an impact, but this time I'm focusing on extra efforts supported by our religious institutions and our faith-based communities. Why? Well, I believe that genuine religious belief has the power to bring us together in ways that go beyond prayer, ritual, or study. It can shake us from our narrow ideas and push us to take a wider view or consider a different approach to getting things done. This book is less about the tenets of our faith (although of course they matter) and more about the many cords that spring from that faith and tie us together in pursuit of a common goal. People and communities of faith play a crucial role in solving the pressing problems of our communities.

A shared sense of purpose, in the end, is the difference-maker in the stories I'm looking to share here.

Oh, I'm all for the lone wolves and self-starters among us who look to make things happen on their own, but I believe that when we invest in the idea of something bigger than ourselves, something bigger than we can perhaps understand, and that when we come together for our greater good, we can't help but surpass our own expectations and along the way find opportunities to celebrate, support, and comfort each other. And it doesn't end there: We're also helping ourselves. Recent studies tell us that active religious practice, such as regular attendance in places of worship and regular observance of ritual and prayer, is directly linked to our mental health. In one such study, as reported recently by *The Wall Street Journal*, Sapien Labs, the information technology company behind the Global Mind Project, concluded that countries with the lowest mental well-being scores are also the countries with the lowest measurable levels of active religious practice. When and where people are spiritually adrift, they tend to be emotionally adrift as well.

We ought to be paying attention to this, too.

I see those reports and worry for our future—you know, because of these perilous times and all. I worry about the slow creep of loneliness and anxiety and depression that seems to find those of us who are already feeling disconnected and untethered, and at some remove from a community of like-minded souls. I worry we are losing our way as a caring, thinking, *feeling* society, where we are too often encouraged to keep to ourselves and watch our backs and look out for our own.

Mostly, I worry about what seems to be a societal tilt away from organized religion, and I am always on the lookout for ways to reverse that trend and help us lean toward the other direction. I want us all to remember that faith *matters* for America, not as a political prop, but as an essential part of our social fabric. That little neighborhood church on the corner isn't just a place to pray or preach. It's a powerful part of what holds us all together.

I guess that's why I had that crazy idea to gather all of those theologians to see whether we might find a way to issue a powerful statement on the importance of religion in a time of such political uncertainty. But in some ways I'm glad we weren't able to come together on this, because it opened the doors for me to imagine a book such as this one—where I am able to show by example the glorious transformation that can happen when a group of like-minded individuals devote themselves to a greater good. I've chosen the following stories so that this book would show, not just tell, the value of our faith communities to our neighborhoods and nation. A picture, as they say, is worth—well, you know.

Let's face it, religion has gotten a bad rap in recent years. A lot of people are turned off by it or think it doesn't have any relevance in their lives. That's a shame. They look at the headlines regarding the transgressions of some of our religious leaders and our religious institutions and think that all of our leaders are hypocrites. They report that organized religion is too regimented, too set in its ways—ways that no longer seem relevant in today's world. This, too, is a shame. Also, it's not true, and this book is just one way I hope to redirect that type of thinking. Because when you read the stories of hope and faith and healing I chronicle and see how people all over the country are coming together with the support of their religious institutions and faith-based communities, you'll see something special. Timeless. Essential. It's eye-opening, really—a revelation, if you will—and I consider it a blessing to be able to share these accounts in this way.

Yes, at the center of the stories in the following chapters are the bighearted efforts of one or two determined, compassionate individuals, but beneath those big, beating hearts you will also find the firm foundation of religious community. There will be strength (and safety!) in numbers. There will be mutual support. And, at bottom, there will be the exponential lift that happens when a faith-based institution helps a congregant or neighbor realize a vision.

The way I see it, taking on an activist role or looking to become an agent of change is a lot like running a political campaign. You can start out working it from your living room, but you're not likely to get anywhere unless you have a campaign team working with you, from a campaign headquarters. Basically, you need a club-house, like a lot of us used to have as kids. You need a team, a place to belong. And, on a purely practical level, you need somewhere you can all hang out, exchange ideas, and bring in people who share your vision and your passion for whatever it is you're trying to accomplish. That's the role our religious institutions are providing in their communities these days, and I'm tremendously excited about it.

And it's not just me. A lot of the religious leaders I talk to tell me there are significant numbers of young people coming back to faith—in large part because of the isolation so many of them felt during the worst of the COVID pandemic. (It will be interesting to see how statistics reflect this apparent shift in coming years, as we learn more about the many ways our behaviors were transformed on the back of the pandemic.) They've come to realize that the religious institutions and observances they might have left behind when they moved out on their own had played a significant role in helping them build their sense of self and their sense of community, and they want to get back to it in some way. I'm excited about *this*, too, and it is my hope that these stories inspire young people to become even more involved in their faith communities.

The fundamental purpose of religion, the throughline that runs among almost all the world's major faiths, is love. And when I talk about love, I'm not talking about a Hallmark-card emotion or a romantic notion. It's more about the sense that we are connected to each other, responsible for each other. We are, after all, our brothers' and sisters' keepers, and here I want to introduce readers to a group of folks who take that responsibility seriously—and joyfully.

At its core, this is a book about the institutions of faith and the people who are part of those institutions who have an idea, sometimes even a big idea, about healing and helping and hoping against hope that they might somehow ease the burdens of others. And it's about how these people, through the structures of their religious institutions, are able to turn an idea into something that forms and shapes and lifts a community. You see, I think America needs a revival, a faith revival, to help us understand that we are all connected to one another and that even our most motivated, dedicated souls must lean on the support of those who share their faith and vision to bring about meaningful change.

My goal here is to get readers to think outside themselves for a bit, to think bigger than themselves, to open their hearts to what's possible instead of what's impossible. This book is my way of saying to people who might dismiss the value of faith communities, Hey, before you write these things off, before you decide faith doesn't really have a place in your life, before driving idly by a church or synagogue or mosque in your community without a thought to what might be going on inside, take a look at what some of these folks are doing, empowered by the forward-thinking support of their religious leaders and other members of their congregations. Or maybe you already believe but you need encouragement. That's here, too—and plenty of it.

Why is it on me to share these stories? Well, when you run for president, when you've served nine terms as a congressman and two terms as governor, you meet a lot of people. You see a lot of things. And when you leave office, you continue to engage with people who invariably put you in touch with the engaging people *they* happen to know. After a while, if you keep your eyes open and your ears to the ground, you wind up connecting with a great many people and hearing a great many stories, and it feels to me as though I'm being called to share some of these stories—especially now, in a time when people are always asking me what they can do about the mess we find ourselves in.

What can you do? Well, for starters, you can stand alongside me in being inspired by people who aren't buried by our political headlines or preoccupied with the gnashing of teeth that characterizes a lot of our discourse. These are people who have decided there is something they can do to make the world a better place. Their world. Our world. I'm excited about what they've accomplished and what they are accomplishing still, and thrilled to be able to share their stories with you.

Won't you join me on this journey?

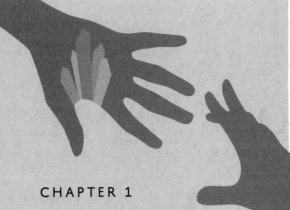

CHAPTER 1

REVEREND ERIC MANNING

Forgiveness

On June 17, 2015, a twenty-one-year-old white supremacist attended a Bible study at the Emanuel African Methodist Episcopal (AME) Church in Charleston, South Carolina—the oldest black church in the South.

I won't mention this young man's name in these pages. He doesn't deserve to be acknowledged in a direct way. It's a name that is now etched in the blood of the victims, but there is no call to give it voice here. (Anyway, you can find this person's name in the god-awful headlines and news accounts from that terrible day.) But I do want to lay out the facts of this heartbreaking story and set the scene for what happened in its aftermath.

At about nine o'clock that night, after participating in the study and joining a dozen African American church members and leaders in reflection and prayer, the young white man abruptly stood and aimed a .45-caliber Glock 41 at an eighty-seven-year-old church member named Susie Jackson. His demeanor turned from warm and searching to chillingly cold and menacing. It was as though a switch had been flipped. When the rest of the group understood what was happening, many of them rose in shock and defiance and tried to talk the young man down from his rage. The shooter responded with defiance of his own and said, "I have to do it. You rape our women and you're taking over our country. And you have to go."

The shooter started shouting racial epithets and announcing that he intended to kill everyone in the room. As he opened fire, Susie Jackson's nephew, Tywanza Sanders, a twenty-six-year-old graduate of Allen University, a private historically black university in nearby Columbia, leaped in front of his aunt and took the first bullet. He would die at the scene, along with his aunt, who was also a member of the church choir; Clementa C. Pinckney, the church's revered pastor and a Democratic member of the South Carolina Senate; Cynthia Graham Hurd, a branch manager for the Charleston County Public Library system and the sister of a former state senator; Ethel Lee Lance, the church's sexton; DePayne Middleton-Doctor, a pastor and school administrator at Southern Wesleyan University; and Sharonda Coleman-Singleton, another pastor, who also worked as a speech therapist and high school track coach. A ninth victim, Daniel L. Simmons, a pastor serving the AME church in the nearby fishing village of Awendaw, would later die at a local hospital.

All nine victims, who would come to be known as "the Emanuel Nine" in headlines across the country, were killed by multiple gunshots fired at close range. And, of course, all nine deserve to be named here, and remembered and honored.

Three other people attending the study—Felicia Sanders, the mother of Tywanza Sanders; his young niece; and a woman named Polly Sheppard—survived the mass shooting, the first two because they had the presence of mind to lie on the floor and pretend they'd already been shot and killed, and Sheppard because the shooter singled her out and said he was going to let her live to tell the story of this rampage.

There were other members of the church in the building, but they were not in the room during the shootings, which lasted about six minutes, after which the shooter fled the scene, but not before his image was captured by the church's security cameras. (He also said he intended to kill himself when he'd completed his shooting spree, but when he pointed the gun to his own head to do so, he discovered he was out of ammunition.) When he was taken into custody the following day, after a witness identified his vehicle with its Confederate flag bumper sticker, law enforcement officials made public a manifesto the young man had published on his website prior to the shooting, which echoed the venomous racial hatred he had been shouting the night before at the Bible study.

Now, most of you reading these words will be aware of this horrific incident. It dominated our news cycle for weeks following the shooting and sparked an impassioned call (yet again!) to put an end to gun violence and to address the root issues of violence and racial hate crimes in America. You certainly don't need me to remind you of the shooting—the deadliest mass shooting in South Carolina history and one of the deadliest racially motivated mass shootings in American history—especially at the start of a book that is meant to signal the good and healing works I'm discovering in religious institutions and organizations all across the country. And yet as I'm leaning in to my work on this book, I'm realizing there is an important lesson to be mined from what happened *after* this awful tragedy. Here, too, you probably don't need me to remind you that in the days immediately following the massacre a number of members of the congregation got together and quite famously and movingly determined to forgive this young man for his actions on that dreadful day. It was remarkable, although if you spend enough time in Southern churches, you might not find it all that surprising. The members of the Emanuel AME congregation did this both as a community and in many cases individually, as several relatives of the people slain spoke at a bond hearing, where the shooter made his first public appearance just a few days after the shooting.

What was especially amazing was that this demonstration of grace and forgiveness came about in an organic way, at a time when the Emanuel community was without its leader. Pastor Pinckney had been the voice of the church, but that voice had been silenced in the slaughter, and yet the congregation somehow managed to stand on its own to sound this all-important, healing call.

"I forgive you," said the daughter of Ethel Lance, the church sexton, as she spoke of her mother. "You took something very precious from me. I will never talk to her again. I will never, ever hold her again. But I forgive you. And have mercy on your soul."

"I acknowledge that I am very angry," offered the sister of DePayne Middleton-Doctor, the local school administrator. "But the one thing that DePayne always enjoined in our family is she taught me that we are the family love built. We have no room for hating, so we have to forgive. I pray God on your soul."

"To heal we must forgive," offered Polly Sheppard, the woman whose life was spared by the shooter so she would live to tell the story. "That's what I've learned. . . . So much hate. Too much. But as scripture says, 'Love never fails.' So I choose love."

And from Felicia Sanders, the mother of the brave young man who took that first bullet, there was this: "You took my love away from me. And since June 17, I've gotten to know you. I know you because you are in my head all day . . . and I forgive you. That's the easiest thing I had to do."

All around the country, people took note—all around the world, even. And, as important, many of us took heart knowing full well that forgiveness is a core Christian value, and that even in the face of such a monstrous act, committed by a disturbed young man who had turned against a group joined with him in communal prayer, snuffing out the lives of so many innocent people committed to each other and to a life of devotion, the capacity of the human heart to show mercy and compassion is a remarkable thing.

All of which takes me to the story I want to tell here—the story of how a pastor named Eric Manning alighted on the AME congregation in Charleston a little more than a year after the shooting and helped the community continue the hard work of healing and forgiving. As it happened, Reverend Manning was leading another AME church in Georgetown, South Carolina, at the time of the massacre. Reverend Pinckney had been a good friend, and so Reverend Manning's thoughts were with both the Emanuel community and the community he had been tasked to serve. Very quickly, however, his focus turned to his own congregation, as the shooting had left church membership on edge, mourning these losses so close to home, worrying for their own safety, and stressing over what our world was becoming.

"Forgiveness is easier said than done," the reverend shares when I reach out to him to discuss his role in the healing of this community, reflecting on the news bulletins that found him from down the coast in Charleston, highlighting the heartening response of Emanuel members. "When you forgive, it's quick. You quickly say it. But then the question is, a week later, a month later, years later, a decade later, are you still carrying that mantle of forgiveness? And, if so, what does it look like? Does it excuse someone, in this case, for this particular act of violence, or for this racist activity?"

Back in 2015, Reverend Manning prayed on these questions from afar, all the while grieving the loss of his own friend, praying for the victims and their families, and tending to the needs of his community. He followed the news developments out of Charleston and looked on with care and concern as the Emanuel community attempted to move forward, at first under the guidance of one of the church's presiding elders, who had been assigned to lead the church on an interim basis.

I can't imagine what a heavy lift that must have been, to guide a community past the weight of such a loss. For a short time, that work had been taken up by the first pastor formally appointed to lead the Emanuel church in the wake of Reverend Pinckney's murder, before the Right Reverend Richard Franklin Norris of the AME's Seventh Episcopal District determined that the Emanuel community was still in need of a guiding hand to lead them past this darkness.

That particular guiding hand, it turned out, belonged to Pastor Manning, who was tapped by the bishop to succeed the first full-time replacement, and he transferred to the Emanuel AME church in the summer of 2016. It wasn't an assignment the pastor had been seeking, and it may or may not have been one he even welcomed, but his calling was simply to serve, and it had been determined that this was where his service was needed.

He had followed the news since the shootings, of course, and kept up on what was happening in the Emanuel community, but only in a once-removed sort of way, so Reverend Manning believed his first order of business was to do a kind of deep dive, learning what he could about the families of the deceased, about those congregants who had somehow managed to survive this mad rampage, about the many twists and turns the trial had taken since the shooter was indicted a month or so following the incident on nine murder charges and three charges of attempted murder. He understood that to connect with these good people he needed to know their suffering, in whatever ways he might.

"That was week one," he says, "meeting with the families. I wanted to introduce myself and say, 'I am here to serve you.' However that might have looked for them. I didn't want to meet for the first time in the church, when they showed up for that first service, or at the trial, which was still ongoing. I wanted to start by building something. By *rebuilding* something."

At the first service, Reverend Manning stood before the congregation and said, "I don't know how to lead you, but God knows how to lead us."

What a great opener, don't you think?

"A lot of people came up to me afterward and said it was such a profound thing to say," the reverend reflects, "but I was just being honest. It's the truth. I did not know how to lead these people, but I trusted that God knew how to lead them. And I understood from talking to the family members that people were struggling with this whole idea of forgiveness. I understood that you have to give people permission to feel however they need to feel. Ergo, again, God knows."

Forgiveness is a tricky business. It can mean different things to different people, at different times in their lives, and it's up to each of us to figure out what it looks like for us. Does it mean that if we're going to pick up that mantle we must now forgive everyone who has ever wronged us in the past, or everyone who might wrong us in the future? Is it a blanket absolution? Or are we able to pick and choose who we are going to forgive, and on what terms?

As I learned more about the pastor's first days and months with the congregation, I wondered whether there was a line from Scripture that spoke into this moment for him, and he immediately pointed me to Luke 23:34: "Father, forgive them; for they know not what they do."

But he also pointed to the words of the Emanuel mourners as a kind of guidepost—specifically, to the comments and testimony that had been offered in the courtroom at the shooter's bond hearing, where this idea of community-wide forgiveness was first given full-throated voice and captured national attention, and to the reflections and reminiscences the family members of the victims shared with him privately as he was getting to know them. It was in these more intimate conversations, he says, away from reporters or cameras, that he came to know the depth of this community's suffering, because it is one thing to understand such pain and suffering intellectually and perhaps even spiritually, yet quite another to understand it on a personal level.

"When I came here in 2016, we had to get up to speed," Reverend Manning says—meaning the entire community, in such a way that they might be able to move forward from the same page. "I went to court with them every day when the trial was taking place," he explains. "I sat with them when the verdict was read. I prayed with them in our own church, and in our neighboring church, and I thought back to an analogy I have often used, the one that imagines this old piece of furniture. Let's say it's over a hundred years old, this piece of furniture, and let's say you take a sledgehammer to it, and then you set about restoring it. It takes time to put it back together. It takes care. You wonder how long it might take, but you're not going to know. You're not ever going to know. You just have to be faithful and steadfast and patient."

One of the learned truths that found its way to Reverend Manning as the faith and steadfastness and patience of his new community were tested was that he would need to find a way to bring joy back into the church. If you've ever been to a service in an AME church, you'll know it can be a joy-filled, roof-raising celebration—and yet there was nothing to celebrate just yet. For the longest time, it seemed, there was nothing to celebrate. But this was where some of that patience kicked in.

"I think it finds you eventually," the pastor considers, speaking of the joy that he knew would invariably announce itself, even after a shared tragedy. "Not necessarily easily, but it finds you. We still have a struggle, and our struggles are always going to be with us. It is indeed a test, but joy comes, and joy is ever present. And I'm thankful for where God has us, not necessarily wallowing in our past, but understanding that our past shows us several things. One, it shows us our rich history. Two, it shows us our spirit of resilience. Three, there's reconciliation. And then four, the spirit of hope to continue to do this work and make things better. It's that hope that inspires me to keep pressing, to keep going."

These days, that inspiration has been focused on an ambitious memorial the church is building on its grounds—the Emanuel Nine Memorial, designed by Michael Arad, an Israeli-American architect who is perhaps best known for his design of the National September 11 Memorial and Museum. Before beginning work on the project, Michael Arad visited with members of the church and listened as they shared stories about the friends and family members they had lost, and he discovered the same hopeful throughline that Reverend Manning recognized during his first days and weeks as pastor. The resulting memorial design, the architect says, is meant to invite "a dialogue between visitor and place, its past and present."

The memorial effort, co-chaired by Pastor Manning, is intended "to bring people together to resolve their differences, reverse hate, end gun violence, and work toward justice with resolute love and compassion."

The idea of forgiveness might rest at the heart of this healing journey, but it's pretty clear that this community's mercy did not resonate with the shooter in any way. Throughout his bond hearing, the ensuing trial, and his sentencing, this troubled young man did not show any signs of remorse. When congregants and family members spoke to him in court, and looked directly into his eyes, he simply stared back at them blankly.

"You like to think that, over time, there'll be some kind of epiphany, or a Damascus sort of experience," the reverend says, referring to the dramatic conversion of the apostle Paul. "You like to think at some point a person will see the error of his ways. But to this day, I don't believe this young man has. And that's another thing we talk about as a community, how hate and racism can be poured into a person over time, and how that hatred can be ingrained in that person. And we might expect them to have that epiphany, and to repent or change their ways, but that's not how it works. And we have to understand that."

As you'll see as you read along in these pages, Reverend Manning's story and the journey to forgiveness that the Emanuel AME community found itself on in the wake of that horrific shooting stand as an outlier among the other stories I've chosen to share in this book. In most of these accounts, you'll meet people inspired by the light of a new idea, bound to get that new idea up and running so that it might make the world a better place, and helped along in their inspiration by the strength of their religious communities. Taken together, these stories are meant to remind us that we can do big things with small strokes, and that we can do even *bigger* things when those small strokes are buttressed by a shared faith.

That's not exactly the case here, but it seems to me that among the many lessons that flowed from this one epic tragedy in this one small church in Charleston, South Carolina, there is the elemental reminder that very often we must rely on our religious leaders to show us the way. Try as we might, we cannot always go it alone, and for many of us that means that our pastors and priests and rabbis and imams must stand as our compass points, our beacons, pointing us ever forward, through every darkness and uncertainty, until we can find a kind of peace.

And so I'm leading with this account because there is indeed something inspiring about the way this one man was determined to heal this broken community—to lend voice and hope to this suddenly voiceless and hopelessly shattered congregation. It was an assignment he didn't seek, but one he certainly rose to when he was called to serve.

Like I said, forgiveness is a tricky business—and here we see that in the hands and heart of this one man, tasked with leading this community through an unthinkable darkness, what matters in the end is not only how forgiveness is given or whether it is received but that it is even considered.

Let's be clear: This kind of forgiveness is radical. It goes against our base human instincts for vengeance and retribution. But in extending this kind of love, which is possible only through faith, there is a sort of healing that takes place. Faith communities, and humble leaders such as Pastor Manning, show us a way that is able to restore dignity, embrace justice, and forestall cycles of violence, all through the remarkable choice to forgive. Think for a moment about the ripple effects that this choice has had. From senseless bloodshed, which never should have happened, a group of strong and brave people of faith showed the potency and grit of their belief—to choose against hatred even when they were hated, to choose to forgive what seems to many of us to be unforgivable.

As we consider the stories to come, I hope this example stays with us—an example of a church and community held together by the strength, unity, compassion, and resilience of its members. These qualities are likely to be found in the churches, synagogues, and mosques on *your* street corner. They are likely to be found in you. Maybe even in me.

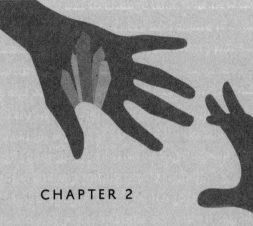

CHAPTER 2

SISTER MARY SCULLION

The Hundred-Million-Dollar Nun

I've never met anyone quite like Sister Mary Scullion—a force of nature out of Philadelphia who has made it her mission to curb homelessness in her city. It's a mission that has become a model for cities across the country, and it is a blessing to be able to spend some time in these pages looking at what she has built, what she is building still.

That *force of nature* description attaches to Sister Mary naturally, almost inevitably. I hear it from everyone I meet who knows her. She's the kind of person who gets things done, whatever it takes. And it just so happens that the thing she's committed her life to doing is solving homelessness.

"None of us are home until all of us are home," she says, looking ahead to her retirement as we visited to interview her for this book, and sounding a line that has become a rallying cry throughout her organization.

After spending just a little bit of time with her and coming to appreciate her commitment to this community, I recognize that this isn't just a line with Sister Mary. It's a core belief—a belief she has fought for consistently throughout her career as an activist and agent of change. She's not just talking about it. She's *doing* it.

Sister Mary is a member of Sisters of Mercy, an international community of Roman Catholic women committed to a life of poverty, chastity, obedience, and service. This last is key, because the first three vows on this list are taken by *all* Catholic sisters, all over the world. But you have to read the fine print here, because it's the vow of service that sets the Sisters of Mercy apart, a vow Sister Mary took very much to heart, going back to when she was a student at Saint Joseph's University, when she first connected with the homeless community in Philadelphia—a community she sometimes refers to as the unhoused, a term that signals a temporary or transitional situation instead of a permanent one, and that pushes us to consider the true meaning of "home."

That connection runs deep—so deep, in fact, that Sister Mary was named by *Time* magazine in 2009 as one of its one hundred most influential people in the world, and in 2011 she was awarded the Laetare Medal, the highest honor given to an American Catholic. (Oh, and let's not forget: She was the commencement speaker at Georgetown University in 2017 and has received honorary doctorates from Georgetown and the University of Pennsylvania.) But she didn't set out to win awards or accolades. No, she set out to make a difference, starting from when she first volunteered at a local soup kitchen while she was still studying at Saint Joseph's University. This led up to a weeklong retreat, under the auspices of the Sisters of Mercy, of living on the streets of Philadelphia, trying to understand firsthand what it meant to be homeless—a retreat Sister Mary embarked on at her own request.

I have a hard time getting my head around this last detail. I mean, can you imagine? It's one thing to work tirelessly on behalf of your city's unhoused population, but to join them, even temporarily? To live on the streets, to walk the walk just so that you might talk the talk and better know the community you're hoping to serve—well, I think that's simply astonishing.

It's the kind of astonishing that has not gone unnoticed in and around Philadelphia, where Sister Mary is pretty much revered. I'm told that when she is out and about in one of the city's neighborhoods where her good works have been most keenly felt, people come out to greet her. They come out as individuals and in large groups. They call her name and cheer her on, as though she's Rocky running up the steps of the Philadelphia Museum of Art. They want to thank her, touch her, connect with her in some way.

When I ask her about this, I suggest that the reason people are responding like this is that they want some of her *godliness* to rub off on them, but Sister Mary quickly disabuses me of that notion and says it's the other way around. "When I see all of *them*," she says, "I see the goodness and godliness all around. I'm looking at something bigger than me."

That weeklong retreat was an eye-opener for Sister Mary—a heart-opener, too. And it got her thinking. In the mid-1980s, she took it upon herself to do her own census of women living on the streets of Philadelphia. It tore at her to see so many untethered, unsheltered women in her hometown, mostly because she couldn't understand why the government, or the community, wasn't doing something about it. How was it that so many of us had become inured to the sight of people sleeping at bus depots, or in train stations, or huddled against the cold in the doorways of storefronts that had been closed for the night? In her survey, Sister Mary got to know women who had fallen through the cracks of any number of city and state social programs, including dozens who had been housed in the state's mental hospitals before they'd been shut down in the 1960s and 1970s.

And she wasn't just out there counting heads. She was getting to *know* these women, each one of them, trying to understand how the system had failed them, what was holding them back, and how she might help them get on a more hopeful course. She knew their names and their stories, and they came to know her as well. They weren't just a problem anymore; they were people, with names and faces and backstories. It got to where Sister Mary couldn't sleep at night knowing that her friends on the streets didn't have a roof over their heads or a decent meal in their bellies.

"I can no longer recall the exact number," she says of the results of her census, "but it was about a hundred or so. It's not like today. There weren't so many people living on the street back then."

No, there weren't—but to Sister Mary just *one* woman living on the street was one woman too many, so she took the results of her census to the city's Office of Mental Health and lobbied for funds and programming to address the issue. She had no idea what kind of reception her push might receive—only that she couldn't look away from the issue and that she wouldn't allow any of the city officials who stood in her way to look away either. Remember, she had walked the walk with many of these same women, and struggled the struggle, so she felt a profound connection to their plight.

"Instead of all the shelters, with their do-not-admit lists, I wanted to establish a safe haven for these women," she explains. "A safe haven where we would just have an admit list. Where our focus would be on housing these women and getting them the necessary health care and all that business."

All that business led to the launch of an organization called Women of Hope, which was able to fill in some of those cracks for a great many of these women. And Sister Mary was right there in the trenches with her charges, living alongside them in the full-service shelter she helped to establish in a building that had once housed a Catholic school. She doesn't say as much when sharing her story, but I believe this was her way of putting it out there that there was dignity to be found inside the walls of these shelters—or, at least, that there was no *indignity* in finding yourself there or in living among other women who might be struggling. If the Women of Hope shelter was good enough to become a home for these women, then it was good enough for her.

My friend Stephen Steinour, the CEO of Huntington Bancshares Incorporated (who for the longest time was a leading philanthropist in Philadelphia and chairman of the Chamber of Commerce for Greater Philadelphia), was one of the first people to introduce me to Sister Mary and to her marvelous work. He was probably also the first person I heard describe her as "a force of nature."

"She cusses, she swears, she spits," Steve says, when I push him to share his impression and help me understand her impact on the city's homeless population. "She's a superstar, a Roman Catholic nun who's not afraid to stand against the church. She's not afraid of anybody. If she didn't think the bishop was doing enough to combat homelessness, she called him on it, and made it her mission to do something about it. She knows how to work with Fortune 500 CEOs, and at the same time is quite comfortable going up to men and women on the street and connecting with them, wherever they are."

Early in the development of Women of Hope, Sister Mary met a woman named Joan Dawson, who at the time was studying accounting at Drexel University. On the face of it, they were an unlikely pair. Sister Mary was living a religious life, bound by her monastic vows, while Joan was living a secular life, focused on her studies. Both were women of faith, however, and this was how they connected. It was a faith in the Lord that allowed them to believe that they could bring about some good in their little corner of the world. That they were meant to do this type of work and that they were meant to do it together. You see, they actually met through the men and women they knew on the street, since Joan and Sister Mary were both working tirelessly to meet the needs of Philadelphia's unhoused community—food, clothing, shelter, medical care.

For each of them, individually, the work was a calling. For both of them, collectively, it was a shared vision—and, soon enough and for the next many years to come, a shared mission. When the two women finally rolled up their sleeves and went to work on this issue, they realized they had a lot of the same ideas on how to make a difference in the lives of the people they were already serving, so they started developing a program of continuing care that they believed would have a more lasting impact than some of the makeshift or stopgap initiatives that had been in place in their hometown of Philadelphia and in cities all over the country. Actually, to call it a "program" is maybe overstating things a bit, because at the outset all they could think about was meeting an immediate need, even if it meant that need would be met only for the next little while.

One of their first orders of business was finding a building that could serve as a shelter, and they looked to the Philadelphia skyline. "That's something we always noticed," Sister Mary says. "Something we always talked about. You'd look out and see all these beautiful municipal buildings, and then at night they'd be locked up with nobody inside. Our people were outside, freezing to death, and there were all these empty spaces all over the city."

These two women set out to change that—however, they didn't have access to any of those grand buildings in the beginning. So what did they do? Well, on one particularly cold night they visited a public building they'd had their eyes on as security guards were locking the place for the evening. Then they pretty much invited themselves inside. Really. They just put their foot in the revolving door out front and refused to move. The poor security guards didn't know what to make of these two feisty, determined women—and to hear Sister Mary recount that moment, it sounds to me as if she surprised even herself with her determination.

"We just told them we were coming in," Sister Mary recalls. "We told them who we were and said we had people who needed a place to stay warm for the night."

How about *that*? This force of nature would not be denied, and all the security guards could do was throw up their hands and let Sister Mary and her group inside. They stayed until seven o'clock the next morning, and by the end of that day Sister Mary and Joan Dawson were negotiating with city representatives for permission to keep using city facilities that winter—and for a more suitable location in another public building.

Eventually, the two women commandeered the locker rooms of one of the city's outdoor swimming-pool facilities—an ideal spot, Sister Mary explains, because the space was already outfitted with showers and bathrooms. "We brought in cots and spread ourselves out, and we parked ourselves there that whole winter. That was the beginning of Project HOME."

There's a lesson, I think, in this beautiful moment of determination. It's a lesson that we can perhaps attach to our own lives, our own circumstances; for when we stand on the side of right, when our cause is just and virtuous and true, we can sometimes bend our societal norms in service of a greater good. Sister Mary knew full well that commandeering this safe space in just this way went against the rules and regulations, but she believed she needed to step outside the lines a little bit in order to be of service to these good people. That's a model we can all follow from time to time as we look for ways to make a difference, even if it means bending the rules (or, for the moment, ignoring them) to achieve a greater good.

Let me tell you about Project HOME. Its mandate is embedded in its name. The *H* stands for affordable housing. The *O*, opportunities for employment. *M*, medical care. And *E*, education. The idea is not *just* to provide shelter or a hot meal. The idea is not *just* to offer first aid or emergency care. The idea is not *just* to help the unhoused think about finding a job, long-term affordable housing, or opportunities for advancement. It's to do all of these things all at once, and to help lift those in need from a place of despair and onto a more hopeful, more purposeful path.

Of course, Sister Mary knew full well that a shared goal of easing the plight of the city's unsheltered population and a few grudging nods from the folks running these grand municipal buildings would take them only so far, for so long. What Project HOME really needed right out of the gate was funding, but Sister Mary was wired in such a way that she could think only about what was right in front of her. She could repurpose an old church and turn it into a women's shelter, as she had done with Women of Hope, relying on donations and volunteers. She could create an emergency shelter in the basement of a grand old building and find a way to overstay her group's welcome for a few nights, then lay claim to an unused municipal pool locker room, as she and Joan were doing in their first winter at Project HOME. But she didn't have it in her just yet to start thinking of a long-term solution to the city's growing homelessness crisis.

"We had no money, nothing except a lot of good friends who would do what they could to help us out," she recalls. "Joan and I knew we needed to establish ourselves as a 501(c) charitable organization and put together a proposal, but we weren't there yet. There were too many people in need, too many people being left out in the cold. There was work to do, so we went out there and did the work. People were looking at me as maybe a little out there, a little unconventional, but they liked what we were doing, and they could see that we were committed to what we were doing, so the Sisters of Mercy reached out to their brother John Connelly and told him he needed to help."

Sister Mary had no idea the Sisters of Mercy were out there making the case on behalf of her mission, but that's what can happen when you're working with the support of like-minded souls. You're not alone. You're not limited to *you*. The whole is often greater than the sum of its parts—it's a cliché, I know, but in every cliché there is some truth, and in this case it was a wonderful truth. Too, the work Sister Mary and Joan were doing with the archdiocese put them in touch with an endless stream of volunteers from the church and a ready supply of goods and services, and attracted a stream of caring volunteers from all walks of life—students, lawyers, and others from local churches and synagogues.

The community was coming around.

John Connelly, a well-known Philadelphia-area philanthropist, took the Sisters of Mercy at their word. Without any kind of formal proposal, and before the organization even had a mission statement, John Connelly wrote Project HOME a check for $100,000. He also sent over a box of chocolates. This was back in 1989. That money became the seed money for the effort going forward—and those chocolates were put to good and immediate use as well.

"That was a nice touch, don't you think?" Sister Mary says, smiling at the sweetness of the memory.

Life *is* like a box of chocolates, I guess. You never know what you'll find when you look inside, and here what Sister Mary and Joan Dawson found was a wellspring of kindness that reached into virtually every aspect of their community.

When they did finally get around to writing a mission statement, they included these lines:

> We believe that all persons are entitled to decent, affordable housing and access to quality education, employment, and health care.
>
> We believe in the transformational power of building relationships and community as the ultimate answer to the degradation of homelessness and poverty.
>
> We believe that working to end homelessness and poverty enhances the quality of life for everyone in our community.
>
> We believe that the critical resources entrusted to us to achieve our mission must be managed honorably and professionally.

In many ways, the work that Joan Dawson and Sister Mary set out to do was a reflection of the values that had been instilled in Sister Mary in childhood.

"When I was little," she remembers, "my mother would talk to me about God, and I would ask her questions. I asked her why all those people let Jesus be nailed to the cross. Why would they stand by and not do something? She was never really able to answer that question, so I kept asking it. In different ways. And in a lot of ways, I'm still asking that same question. Look at what's going on in the world, the people that are unsheltered, the kids who are being abused. Look at the people in jail, or the hostages of Hamas and Israel, the people fighting in Ukraine and Russia. When you look at all of that, you start to think, in some ways, that it's like Jesus being nailed to the cross. And what are we going to do about it? It's the same, you know. We can't just stand by and say, 'It's not my problem.'

"We are part of one human family. We all have different faith traditions, different whatever. But by coming together and working with each other, being with each other, hopefully we can find a connection that's human. It's those human connections that allow us to find ourselves."

Meanwhile, Joan Dawson completed her studies at Drexel and started working full-time for one of the Big Eight accounting firms. She eventually married and started a family, while Sister Mary continued working for the archdiocese and running Women of Hope, and after that first winter commandeering the facilities at the municipal swimming pool, the two women set about looking for a more permanent shelter for their Project HOME initiative.

"The pool opened back up for the summer, so we needed to find another location," Sister Mary tells, but they kept running into one brick wall after another. Either the facility they were targeting was run-down and uninhabitable, or it was located in one of the nicer parts of town and the neighbors bristled at the idea of a shelter being developed in their back yard. Along the way, they ruffled a few feathers, but if you spend any time talking to Sister Mary, you'll know she doesn't mind ruffling a few feathers if it means making a difference in the lives of the people she's hoping to serve.

A kindness from another benefactor helped Project HOME open the doors of a permanent facility—this time from the late Senator John Heinz of Pennsylvania, who had long supported the mentally ill, the homeless, the disabled, and the disenfranchised. With the senator's help, Project HOME was able to collect Section 8 approvals for the development of the housing units that would be built on the upper floors of a building the two women had found that was in foreclosure—a commercial property on Fairmount Avenue in downtown Philadelphia that they hoped would accommodate individual living units on the upper floors and a café, thrift store, and bookstore on the ground floors, which would provide employment opportunities for the shelter's permanent residents.

And yet the assist from Senator Heinz didn't allow Project HOME to open its doors all the way, because here again the neighbors pushed back, stalling the organization's efforts to open up the residential floors of the building.

"This whole NIMBY thing was an issue for us," Sister Mary shares. "NIMBY, as in 'not in my back yard.' It's the kind of thinking that gets in the way of a lot of the good works organizations like Project HOME hope to accomplish in our communities. These problems don't exist in a vacuum. They are not hypothetical. These are real people, in real need, and they just happen to be living next door."

Soon, the building was tied up in a lawsuit, which allowed Project HOME to operate its ground-floor commercial operations but put a halt on the opening of the residences. It was an unfortunate turn Sister Mary might have anticipated if she hadn't been expecting the good in people to help her get past the bureaucratic red tape. These days, the area surrounding that Project HOME development on Fairmount Avenue is one of the nicest neighborhoods in the city, but back then it was just starting to gentrify, and there was a feeling that the opening of a shelter in the heart of that community might dampen what was becoming a hot real estate market.

Sister Mary and Joan Dawson (soon to be Joan McConnon) were relentless, taking their fight to the state supreme court and to the US Justice Department. Sister Mary even got herself arrested, protesting the courts' indecision.

(This wasn't her first run-in with the law, by the way: She was also arrested for civil disobedience for giving food to the homeless without a permit at Thirtieth Street Station.)

"They were holding our building hostage," she says. "It was like a political prisoner."

Ultimately, Project HOME won a landmark court decision, paving the way for fair housing rights for persons with disabilities and opening the doors on the much-needed residences on the upper floors of their first building.

Perhaps my favorite Sister Mary story was shared with me by my friend Scott Jenkins, who's known her for a number of years through his work on the board of the Connelly Foundation. Scott tells of the time Project HOME made application to the Department of Health and Human Services (HHS) to become one of twenty-five federally qualified health centers (FQHCs) in the country. When the list came out on a Friday and Project HOME wasn't on it, she started working the phones and beating the drums, and making all kinds of noise on behalf of her application, despite the fact that the folks at HHS had already weighed in with their decision. She even reached out to Pennsylvania senators Bob Casey and Arlen Specter, and also to Joe Biden, who was a senator at the time representing the neighboring state of Delaware.

She'd already made the case to HHS, but here she was making it again—well past the eleventh hour. But that's the kind of passion and determination she brought to this mission. She would not be denied. And—wouldn't you know it?—HHS came out the next week with a press release announcing that Congress had approved funding for an additional group of FQHCs, and this time around Project HOME made the cut. Scott Jenkins and I have taken to calling Sister Mary the Hundred-Million-Dollar Nun, because that's how much money she's raised over the years for her various Project HOME initiatives—and she's confident that even in retirement she'll find a way to help the organization meet its ever-changing goals.

Sister Mary herself sums up her fundraising strategy better than I can here: "First, identify the problem," she says. "Then find a way to connect the people in need with others who want to make a difference. You never know where the grace from that interaction will lead."

To illustrate, she tells me that it was our mutual friend Stephen Steinour who connected her with Leigh and John Middleton, two great Philadelphia-area philanthropists (John's the owner of the Philadelphia Phillies), who were inspired to get involved and make a transformational $25 million gift that exponentially expanded Project HOME's capacity to build housing. Too, it was John Connelly who connected Sister Mary with Lynne and Harold Honickman, of The Honickman Foundation, which helped to open the doors for Project HOME into the city's Jewish community and helped to make a strategic difference in its work and mission, offering a living, breathing example of Martin Luther King Jr.'s vision of a beloved community, where there is no such dynamic as "them and us," where there is only "us".

But money and networking alone won't solve the problem. Sadly, there are more homeless people living on the streets of our American cities today than there were when Sister Mary first started working on this issue. Among our ten largest cities, Philadelphia possesses the highest poverty rate, and yet, of these same ten cities, it has the lowest number of people living on the streets, although these encouraging numbers don't account for the great many individuals who are "doubled-up," living as two or three or four families in a single-family unit, or who are couch surfing and living like nomads, bouncing from one friend's or family member's apartment to another.

Still, Project HOME has had an enormous impact. And Sister Mary is confident that, even after her retirement later this year, the organization will remain a thriving full-service agency addressing the root causes of homelessness, dedicated to empowering individuals to break the cycle of homelessness. They've developed more than 1,000 units of affordable and supportive housing across nineteen residences. In addition, the organization maintains 144 units of recovery-focused housing intended to serve individuals recovering from drug and alcohol addiction, as well as that eleventh-hour health center Sister Mary helped to push over the goal line as the clock ran out.

She's confident, too, that homelessness is a solvable problem in our society. "Not because of programs like Project HOME," she says, "but because we are able to put good public policy in place to address the issue." To hear Sister Mary tell it, good public policy can provide access to programs, health care, educational and training opportunities, fair wages, and affordable housing.

"We've lost thirty percent of affordable housing units in the last ten years," she notes, "but that just means we need to build new ones, while preserving the ones we have. It's like musical chairs. It's just math. But if we have the political will, if we have people working together across the public and private sectors, we can make a difference.

"Recovery is in our mission statement," she continues. "The Sisters of Mercy are why we're here today. The archdiocese is why we're here today. People of faith like the Connellys, the Honickmans, the Middletons, and especially the women and men who found the courage and grace within to get up and try again, they're why we're here today. Yes, faith is very much a part of our work, but what's been really beautiful about the way Project HOME has grown is that we are a community of people from all walks of life. We have really strong Jewish support. We have really strong Muslim support, and of course we have really strong support among Christians, especially among Presbyterians, Episcopalians, Methodists, and all that. It's really powerful, and really amazing, and it's all a part of who we are and what we've become."

As of this writing, Sister Mary is able to look back at an enduring legacy built on a strong spiritual conviction and an abiding belief in the dignity of every person her organization serves, as well as every person who is of service. One of the initiatives she's most proud of, she shares, is the inspirational meeting Project HOME holds every Tuesday morning at nine thirty.

Here, I'll let Sister Mary have the last word and tell you all about it:

"We're now operating at twenty-two sites, so we do this meeting virtually and in person. People can connect by phone or Zoom or whatever. And it happens every Tuesday at the same time, so we get alums, former staff members and volunteers, whoever wants to join. Someone shares two or three minutes of something that impacted them that week, or inspired them that week, and I might say a few words or we'll hear from another member of our executive team. There's something very spiritual about it, but we don't preach or ask that everyone pray. That's for each of us to do on our own. We want to reinforce for our people that they are responsible for developing their own spirituality, just as I am responsible for developing mine, and when we come together, we learn from each other what spirituality is. It doesn't matter who you are or what you are, only that I have something to learn from you and that you probably have something to learn from me."

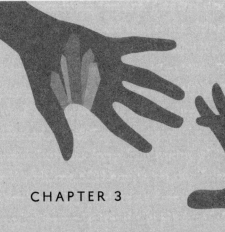

CHAPTER 3

REVEREND JOSEPH F. MAIOCCO III

Keeping the Lights On

Community is a funny thing, don't you think? Belonging, too. It's hard for me to describe what it is that makes me comfortable when I visit a new place or meet a bunch of new people, what it takes for me to feel like I've been counted in. It's one of those I'll-know-it-when-I-see-it type of deals.

That's how I feel about St. John's Episcopal Church in Naples, Florida, where I have definitely come to know it. How my wife, Karen, and I wound up at St. John's is kind of interesting, and it started because we vacation in Naples, and when we're away from home, we always look for a place of worship on Sundays. The moment we set foot in St. John's, we felt like we belonged. We liked the service, the music, the people. Mostly, we liked the minister, the Reverend Joseph F. Maiocco III, who struck me as a talented communicator and someone with a deep and abiding passion for the community he was serving.

Father Joe has a way of rolling out the welcome mat and making you feel like you've been part of the church all along. I liked him straightaway. Plus, I would soon learn that he had spent some time in my part of the world, having started out as a youth adviser in the Diocese of Pittsburgh, not too far from my hometown of McKees Rocks, Pennsylvania, and then later on serving as the rector of Advent Episcopal Church in Cleveland, so I think I picked up on some of that hometown flavor. But it went deeper than that, because Father Joe had lived a life of service in almost every sense of the term, serving as a navy chaplain at Pearl Harbor and through tours of duty during Operation Desert Shield and Operation Desert Storm. His commitment to lifting others on the back of the Lord's

Word and pursuing his ministry in far-off places, in unconventional and selfless ways, was hard not to notice and admire.

And yet I probably wouldn't have thought of highlighting his good works in these pages until Hurricane Ian made landfall in southwestern Florida in late September 2022, with Category 4 winds causing a catastrophic storm surge that threatened to wipe St. John's off the map. Mercifully, the church weathered the storm, but not before it was tossed and turned every which way. Keep in mind, this was just five years after another Category 4 storm, Hurricane Irma, made landfall a few miles south of Naples, setting in motion the largest evacuation in the state's history. And just a little more than two years after the world was effectively shuttered by the pandemic—an adversity the St. John's community wasn't alone in facing, but an adversity just the same.

Just to be clear, I would have thought of Father Joe for a bunch of other reasons, and I would have counted myself fortunate to be a visiting member of his community, but the way he was able to move about that community in the wake of Ian's devastation, and Irma's disruption, and COVID's uncertainty was truly inspiring—and, so, he rates a mention here.

(Absolutely, he rates a mention here!)

It was an inspiration born of desperation, because Naples was hit hard by that 2022 storm. Hurricane Ian made national news, but at the local level it was ruinous—the costliest weather disaster on record worldwide. People lost their homes, cars, businesses— everything. It was awful. The St. John's campus was essentially underwater. The sanctuary and the two main outbuildings were flooded. It was a challenge for Father Joe and his wife, Janet, to get to the church on the morning after the storm. A drive that normally took them just a few minutes took more than an hour. Most of the roads in town were closed, blocked by fallen trees and downed power lines, and as they made their way to the church, they were struck by the destruction all around—and so they braced for the worst.

"We had to go this way, and then that way," Father Joe remembers. "The whole way there, we were just hopeful we'd be able to make it to the church. We had no idea of the extent of the storm surge on our property, no idea what we were facing, so we were hopeful that there wasn't any real damage."

But, of course, the damage was very real. And extensive. It turned out, the storm surge wasn't just water from the Gulf. The church was flooded by wastewater as well, and when Father Joe was finally able to slosh his way inside, he was overwhelmed by the smell. That was the first thing he noticed, and the one thing he remembers vividly from his initial inspection. "This is Florida," he explains, "and it can get hot and humid, and it really stunk. I'll never forget that smell. And I'll never forget the picture that found us on that first day. There were desks all over the place, and chairs, and mud. We even found fish in the sanctuary. It was worse than we ever imagined. It felt to us, in that moment, that everything had been destroyed."

The *fish in the sanctuary* detail struck me when Father Joe told me about it later—in part because of the symbolism of the "Jesus Fish" icon, or ichthus, which has come to represent the spread and unity of Christianity, but also because it's such a visual, visceral reminder of the fierce nature of the storm, the devastation the St. John's congregation was now facing, and the wellspring of hope at the heart of the church's restoration. I mean, just close your eyes and picture it: There were fish on the altar! I can't think of a more stirring reminder of Jesus Christ's desire that we are all meant to be "fishers of men" (Matthew 4:19).

Initially, it appeared that the community would never dig its way out from under. What was especially devastating was the fact that the church had recently finished a yearslong renovation project begun in 2008, soon after Father Joe joined the parish. That project had taken on a life of its own, as one repair led to another and then another. Father Joe estimates that, all told, the church had spent approximately $1.2 million on the renovation, which included the construction of a new playground and the rehabilitation of the sanctuary and offices. The punch-list items and finishing touches had just been completed the year before Ian hit, so the buildings and grounds still had that "new car" smell, thirteen years after the renovation work had begun.

Father Joe's first thought, he tells me now on the happy end of a not-so-happy emergency restoration project that would take another year to complete and eat up another $900,000 or so of church funds, was that all of that initial money had been washed away by the storm. And what wasn't *washed away*, in a literal sense, was carried to the curb by Father Joe and his hearty team of volunteers, whose first order of business was to haul away the debris that had been left behind by the storm. It was, as you might imagine, backbreaking work, but it was also heartbreaking, because with each load they carried, there was a meaningful memory and a sense that something irreplaceable was being lost. Still, it wasn't able to break Father Joe's spirit or the spirit of his volunteer army. In fact, it was in this digging out from under that it was decided they would find a way to hold services that Sunday—no small thing considering the wreckage all around.

"In the day or two after the storm, there was this tremendous sense of death," Father Joe recalls. "That's really what it was like for us, a death. We were all grieving what had happened to the building. But what we all realized, almost immediately, is that the strength of our community is not the church itself. It's not the building. It's the people. A lot of times, coming out of one of these disasters, the human community is forged on a much deeper, much more powerful level. That's the invitation I think we all felt from God's Spirit, to come together in a whole new way."

Karen and I happened to be in town a couple of weeks after the hurricane, and we showed up at Sunday-morning services during our visit not realizing the extent of the damage. We knew how hard Naples had been hit, of course, but we naively thought the church was far enough inland and on sufficiently high ground that it had been spared the worst of the storm, so when we arrived and were ushered away from the sanctuary to where services were being held outside, we were surprised.

And, once the full story was made clear to us, uplifted.

As it happened, the St. John's community came together on the very first Sunday after the storm—on the patio. Of course, it helped that this was Florida in September, so they could count on mild temperatures, but I have a feeling they would have been out there praying, singing, communing even in the freezing cold. And they haven't missed a Sunday since. In those first weeks after the hurricane, there was a funeral on the patio, and a baptism, and a wedding. Life went on, through any number of pastoral moments, and Father Joe reports that there was this palpable sense of purpose that ran through the community. Whatever they were celebrating, or mourning, there was this underlying conviction that they were continuing a great tradition, all the while building something new and coming together through this unforeseeable hardship and being there for each other.

We've all heard some version of the mantra that holds that most of our successes in life can be achieved simply by showing up and making an effort, and here our adopted church community was offering a shining example of this truth. What strikes me now, looking back at how the church responded to this disaster, is that the individuals within this community, from Father Joe on down, were showing up not for themselves but for each other—a reminder to us all that a shared hardship is only a small hurdle when it finds us on the road to a shared future.

Remarkably, St. John's didn't miss a beat on Father Joe's watch after Hurricane Ian, and what moved me most about it was the powerful signal it sent to the church community. It put it out there that they would not be chased from their home, that they would not be denied—indeed, that they would survive and get through these trying times together.

"It spoke to me," Father Joe says, "this need to hold services like we always do. It said to me, 'Hey, we might be down, but we're not out.' And I knew it would give people hope. A lot of our people, in those first days after the storm, they weren't even sure we were going to meet, but they came anyway. Maybe they hadn't received the email we sent out, because they'd lost their electricity or the wi-fi was down, so they just showed up hoping we would be there, and we were."

As it happened, one of the church's biggest annual fundraising events was scheduled for the second week of December, just a couple of months after the storm, during which St. John's hosts a dozen or so ministry partners, and Father Joe rallied the troops and made it a priority to see that the event went off as planned. He knew these other organizations were counting on the contributions to that fundraiser, and Father Joe didn't want to let them down, even though his own church was still down for the count.

"Our needs were great, but that didn't discount the needs of the community," he explains. "People needed food at the food banks. They needed medical assistance. Something as simple as getting diapers for their children, or offering assistance to immigrant families, to help them get the necessary support or to improve their English. All of these essential programs and services need funding, and we were determined to meet those needs, despite the needs we were facing on our campus."

This, to me, is perhaps the most compelling example of the strength of the church's commitment to service—not *just* to the continuity of keeping their own services going, but also (and perhaps even *mostly*) to helping to keep the lights on beyond their church community.

"I knew our ministry partners needed us now more than ever," Father Joe reflects on that uncertain time in the wake of Hurricane Ian. "They were counting on our support, and we would not let the storm keep us from our commitments."

That fundraising event ended up generating nearly $200,000 in support, eclipsing Father Joe's goals and redoubling the community's commitment to the important work of the church that went beyond the rebuilding of the church itself.

Meanwhile, Father Joe went into damage-control mode. One of the things they don't always teach you in seminary is how to run a business, which is what many church leaders are asked to do once they step to the pulpit. That can mean managing a budget, hiring staff, overseeing building maintenance, and on and on, and here it worked out that Father Joe had learned a thing or two during that protracted renovation. He also knew that with this kind of water damage he needed to act within the first forty-eight hours to ensure that the walls of the sanctuary and the outer buildings didn't develop mold, or otherwise deteriorate, and that the structures would be salvageable.

Father Joe even knew to anticipate this "unforeseeable" hardship, in what ways he could, because the storm had been in the forecast for weeks leading up to the moment of landfall. He had already registered the church with a remediation group and directed the church's maintenance crew to lay in sandbags around the property—two precautions he'd never taken before—although in the end neither safeguarding effort paid dividends. St. John's was on the fifth page of the remediation waiting list for area institutions and businesses seeking aid, and the sandbags did little to stop the flooding, but at least Father Joe could tell himself (and his community) that he'd done everything he could as Naples braced for the storm.

"Hurricanes are so unpredictable," he says. "It can be such a capricious storm. You just never know what you're facing until you're facing it. Originally, this storm was supposed to go up to Tampa, and we were supposed to just get a light brushing. The forecasts all said we were going to be okay. But you have to be prepared, right?"

As he and his wife left the church property on that first day following the storm, they happened by a Servpro truck in the neighborhood. Father Joe took it as a sign, that these saviors had alighted on his path, and he quickly got on the phone with a Servpro representative to arrange for an inspection. Servpro is a national chain of restoration and remediation professionals, with a team of emergency cleanup and construction crews ever at the ready, and the company was able to get a team to the St. John's campus the very next day—and the very next day after *that* there was a crew of forty to fifty workers on-site ready to begin.

It turned out, the Servpro team was a godsend, and if Father Joe hadn't flagged them down early on in the crisis, St. John's would have had to take its place in line, but because he reached out early, the restoration crew was able to start work immediately. The restoration would go on for months, and it didn't exactly go smoothly—not least because it looked for a while that the church property would be condemned, based on the FEMA guidelines that stipulated that rebuilding costs that exceeded 50 percent of a property's value would not be approved under federal insurance guidelines.

Happily, there was no shortage of capable handymen and handywomen in the St. John's community to help out with the heavy lifting and to fill in where the Servpro team didn't quite reach, including painting and light plumbing and electrical work, and as he walked me through the story of those dark days just after the storm, I could still hear the emotion in his voice, more than a year and a half later.

All along, Father Joe tried not to think about money or what this emergency renovation project was costing the church. All he could think about, really, was what it would cost his community if they didn't go forward with all of these repairs in a timely fashion—and what it would cost them if they used up *all* their available funds to pay for the infrastructure instead of underwriting the programs needed to support that infrastructure. One day he looked up and realized he was spending most of his time dealing with insurance companies and local ordinances and trying to stretch the church's resources to cover the mounting cost of repairs, and that he was prioritizing the wrong things.

"Our end goal in life is not to amass a larger and larger endowment," he says of his focus on church finances during this crisis. "Our end goal is to use whatever financial blessings we receive to be a blessing to people who are in need in our community. We were hoping to get some money from FEMA to go toward the estimates we were getting from these contractors, and we continued to fund our ministry partners to support all these other programs we had going on. The renovation was a priority, but it wasn't our *only* priority."

All this time later, he looks back on the aftermath of Hurricane Ian, Hurricane Irma, and the COVID pandemic as one teachable moment after another . . . and another. "One of the great takeaways for me is that I'm really not in control as much as I'd like to be," he says, reflecting on those low, low moments after that terrible storm surge. "I might have a great plan, but a lot of times that plan is affected by events you just don't see coming. Control is an illusion. That's what a storm like Ian can teach you. What a storm like Irma can teach you. What COVID can teach you. There's nothing wrong with planning, with being organized, with going through your life a certain way, but I've learned to be flexible. To let go. To surrender to the serendipity of life."

Oh, and speaking of planning, Father Joe is in the habit of planning his sermons several weeks in advance, and it worked out that the service he'd organized for that first Sunday after the hurricane was going to feature a closing hymn called "Wind, Wind, Blow on Me." The church bulletin had been printed, and nobody really thought anything of it, until they all started singing. "Wind, wind, blow on me / Wind, wind, set me free / Wind, wind, my Father sent the blessed Holy Spirit."

"We all joked that God really has a sick sense of humor," Father Joe says, looking back on that moment on the patio when the community gathered for the first time after the storm. "There we were, the whole campus was destroyed by this Category 4 windstorm, if you will, and we're all singing 'Wind, wind, blow on me.' It was just incredible. Of course, we had to laugh."

One of the most serendipitous aspects of the recovery effort at St. John's was an initiative Father John borrowed from a restoration he threw in on at a local YMCA some years earlier, after the gymnasium was struck by lightning and burned to the ground. At the time, Father John handed out Sharpie markers to the community of volunteers who had gathered to help in the rebuilding effort, many of them younger members of the community who had regularly used the gym. He asked the volunteers to write their favorite Bible verses onto the floorboards beneath the basketball court or onto the bare walls that had been readied for painting.

Such a creative, community-building exercise, don't you think? And a great way to layer in those all-important points of connection that are essential to any rebuilding effort. In fact, it was such an effective exercise that Father Joe dusted it off again here, after the walls of the St. John's sanctuary had been stripped to the studs. This time around, he called the exercise "holy graffiti," and he invited all those who had been helping out with the reconstruction, as well as any church members who wanted to leave an indelible mark on the renovated structure, to do the same.

Father Joe took part in the exercise himself, offering this verse from Isaiah 40:31 as his contribution: "But they that wait upon the Lord shall renew their strength; they shall mount up with wings as eagles; they shall run, and not be weary; and they shall walk, and not faint."

He also reached for a line or two from Job when he noticed an empty patch of wall that needed filling: "Though he slay me, yet will I trust in him" (13:15).

"There was a real sense of death in our community as we came together on this," he shares. "There was such tremendous loss, all around. People were losing their homes and forced to live in their cars, and I thought by inviting everybody to share their thoughts in this way, to find these lines from Scripture that were important to us, to each of us in our own way, and to etch them onto the building itself, it would be a very powerful reminder of the importance of keeping our faith."

What I love about this exercise is the way Father Joe was able to get folks thinking of the church's mission, which he knew was written in some way on the hearts of its members. With his "holy graffiti" outreach effort, he was making sure it would also be written on the walls of their renovated buildings, and beneath the floorboards, and that the human connection forged on the back of this string of disasters would take on more lasting shape.

"In the putting back together again, we've become a different people," he reflects. "We all have parts of our lives, hardships, we wouldn't choose to go through again, but often when we look back on those difficult moments, they're probably some of the most important, most informative moments, and we don't want to let go of them."

As I write this, I'm afraid Father Joe and his St. John's congregation are facing down another looming weather disaster—Hurricane Milton, a Category 5 hurricane that, in the first week of October 2024, is threatening to undo all the repair work necessitated by the previous storms.

So, of course, I call him up to see how he's doing, and I catch him as the entire Naples area is making ready for Milton's anticipated landfall. He's just finishing up work with an army of contractors and volunteers, laying in sandbags around the church property and moving irreplaceable items to higher ground.

What's surprising to me, and heartening, is the good cheer I hear in Father Joe's voice as we speak. I mean, he's facing down another storm that, at the moment, looks like it might even be *more* disastrous than the previous storms, but he trusts that all will be made right on the other side of whatever it is that's about to happen.

"We're doing everything we can," he says, "but we'll be back afterward to clean up. Whatever happens, we'll be here."

A postscript: Thankfully, St. John's was spared the worst of the storm. Father Joe sent around an email to the St. John's family the morning after Hurricane Milton made landfall, as Floridians across the state were surveying the damage to their own homes and communities, and he reported that the church had been mostly spared by the ripping winds and surging floodwaters.

"St. John's campus is beautiful, and God has blessed us in restoring it twice," he wrote. "It is our responsibility to preserve this bastion of worship and beauty to the best of our ability."

It is, as we now know, a responsibility he holds dear.

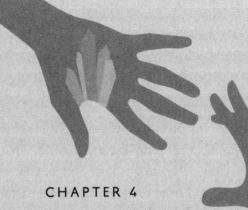

CHAPTER 4

LISA LIBERATORE

Building Community

Like a lot of parents, Lisa Liberatore and her husband, Dimitri Kessaris, worried about the paths their children might take in adulthood: how they'd navigate the world, what kind of work they might do, where they might live. I know that when our girls were little, Karen and I used to have long conversations wondering what their lives might look like as they got older and how we'd be able to help them make good choices along the way.

For Lisa and Dimitri, those conversations were complicated by the fact that their youngest son, Michael, had been diagnosed on the autism spectrum. It's tough enough to worry over the paths your children might walk as they lean in to adulthood; I can't imagine the weight of that worry when you have a child on the spectrum. In Lisa's case, she and her husband were able to lean on the support of their church community, but at the outset that support could touch them only emotionally or spiritually. Logistically, they were still facing an uncertain path.

Michael was diagnosed when he was two and a half years old. His older brother Alexander didn't talk until he was about two, so Lisa didn't think much of it when Michael turned two and wasn't yet speaking. Alexander had gone from zero to sixty in nothing flat and started speaking in full sentences almost immediately after uttering his first words, but Michael was stuck, and when he was finally diagnosed and they knew what they were facing, Lisa and her husband determined to give their son every opportunity to thrive.

Here I started to write that this was "easy enough" when Michael was little—but, as we can all imagine, there's nothing easy about parenting a child on the spectrum. There's one challenge after another—challenges you learn to anticipate and challenges you don't see coming. There's no denying, however, that there are some tremendous programs in place to support children like Michael in a public-school setting. Early on, when they were living in Manhattan, Lisa and Dimitri had a couple of stops and starts at a couple of different schools as they struggled to find an appropriate program for Michael. Nothing seemed to fit or click. Eventually, they found a school in Brookville, New York, that seemed ideally suited to Michael's particular circumstance, so they moved from the city to a nearby town on Long Island and counted their blessings as their son settled into a nurturing, nourishing school environment, where they had every reason to think he would remain until he aged out at twenty-one years old.

That *aging out* business was a big deal. It was one of the challenges Lisa knew to anticipate, but for the longest time she and her husband weren't ready to face it. At first this was something Lisa thought she and her family would have to confront on their own, but as her son's needs became more apparent, and as her connection to her faith and to her church deepened, she realized they would not be alone in this.

The story immediately reminded me of a woman named Loretta Nagle, one of the heroes I visited with when I was researching my book *Courage Is Contagious*. Loretta was one of the founders of Angels' Place, a Christ-centered group home in suburban Detroit for individuals with intellectual and developmental disabilities. Loretta was working as a nurse when she was inspired by the plight of one of her nursing colleagues who was confronting the challenges of raising a disabled daughter and worrying endlessly about what would happen to that child when her parents were no longer able to care for her.

It also reminded me of the drumbeat of concern that found me as governor when I kept hearing from parents of children on the spectrum who were frustrated that their medical insurance wouldn't cover applied behavioral analysis (ABA) therapy, an indispensable tool in the treatment of autism spectrum disorder. As I studied the issue, I came to share their frustration, so we made it a priority to arrange for coverage for state employees affected by this issue, to help them with their child's daily routines.

Lisa and Dimitri were facing some of the same daunting challenges with their son Michael, and they could hear the same clock ticking in their own household, knowing the time would come when they would have to find meaningful ways to fill their son's days and to confront their uncertain future as a family. And yet, like a lot of parents in a similar spot, they were happy that their child's needs were being met for the time being.

Meanwhile, Michael followed in his older brother's footsteps in what ways he could, and their relationship began to stamp the life of their family.

"Alexander was his brother's best mentor and role model," Lisa reflects. "When Alexander wanted to be an altar server, Michael followed right behind him. And then, when Alexander started rowing in high school, Michael showed an interest. He literally ran into the water, so we helped our local rowing team start an adaptive rowing program, and Michael started rowing competitively. It was such an important part of his development, and what we learned was that if we let Michael be guided by his older brother, if they could manage to pursue their shared interests, we would be okay. What we also learned was that if we kept our expectations high, if we believed in him, Michael would find a way to meet those expectations."

And, so, they kept their expectations high, and the two brothers continued to do most everything together, but, at the same time, Lisa worried. More and more, she worried. It got to where she found herself sitting at a holiday show at Michael's school, watching her son singing and dancing and laughing with his friends, when she caught herself wondering what all of these students would do when they aged out of the program. The students were all about nineteen and twenty years old. They'd been together, most of them, for as long as Lisa could remember. She looked around the room at all of *their* parents and knew they were all thinking the same thing, trying not to stress over how the rest of their lives might look or where they might go from here.

Those challenges she wasn't quite ready to face? They were just around the corner. The support she knew she would find within her church community? It was just waiting to be tapped.

Around this time, Michael started showing an interest in cooking. He wasn't able to make an entire meal, but he could work with his mother and help with the prep, and he really seemed to enjoy it. Lisa says he was a natural. Soon, Michael was at his mother's side in the kitchen for every holiday or family gathering chopping and organizing and being a great help, and after a while Lisa looked to keep a good thing going and signed up the two of them to volunteer to cook at their Greek Orthodox church in Southampton, where there was a big industrial-sized kitchen and a steady calendar of events requiring a great many helping hands.

It was the first of the very many tangible resources that would soon open up for Michael at the church.

The more they volunteered, the more Michael seemed to shine, so Lisa arranged for a chef who had recently graduated from a local culinary school to work with him in the kitchen to help hone his skills, and after a while that got Lisa thinking of starting a home-based business where Michael could put his passion for cooking to work in a sustainable way. Together they settled on the idea of making granola and selling it directly to consumers, packaged in gift baskets for special occasions.

"Granola was perfect, really," Lisa reflects. "I mean, there were no knives involved. It was mostly measuring, mixing, packaging. We could get his friends involved as the business grew. We could get our chef involved, the one who'd been working with Michael, and she was inspired to create an original gluten-free recipe for us, with organic ingredients, that tasted amazing. Everybody loved it, and when they found out it was made by these young adults on the spectrum, they loved it even more, and what my husband and I loved about it most of all was that Michael was really committed to it."

Getting Michael started down this path could have easily been a full-time job for his mother, but Lisa already had a full-time job. She was an ear, nose, and throat doctor with a busy practice, yet she managed to dedicate one day each week to overseeing the granola project from her home kitchen, and when one of her patients mentioned that she worked with a nonprofit in Long Island City called Entrepreneur Kitchen, Lisa was all over it. As it happened, there was a dedicated gluten-free space at Entrepreneur Kitchen that wasn't being used, so Lisa worked it out to set up operations there. She also reached out to Michael's school to see whether there were any recent graduates who might have expressed a love for cooking, because she knew she would have to ramp up production, and because she wanted to be able to provide a similar opportunity for other families with young-adult children on the spectrum. With this idea of growing the business in mind, she stopped in at a store across the street from her office that supported local businesses with farm-to-table type products, making sure to bring in some of Michael's granola for the owner to try.

"I told him what we were doing, and he just loved the idea, so I left him some samples," Lisa tells, "and when he got back to me, he said he wanted to carry the granola in all twenty of his stores. I said, 'Twenty stores! We don't have the ability to deliver to twenty stores!' But the owner just said to deliver our granola to his commissary, and he would take it from there."

While all of this was happening, Lisa helped Michael design a website and develop a brand identity for their product. They decided to call the business Luv, Michael, and she got Michael to sign his name to the label in a way that looked like he was giving his customers a gift—you know, signed "Luv, Michael."

Meanwhile, Lisa *still* wasn't ready to face the idea of Michael living on his own, but she knew that finding a productive way for him to fill his days, and perhaps even earn a modest salary, was a first step in this direction. She believed one would follow from the other.

The business exploded, and soon Lisa started hearing from other parents who were starting to hear the same ticking clock announcing the time that *their* children would age out of school. (See what I mean about that *aging out* concern? It finds every family living with autism before too long.) She also heard from a man with a nephew on the spectrum who was developing a group home for individuals with autism, in partnership with a local church. Lisa was excited about what that idea could mean for Michael, but at the time, with everything else she had going on, she didn't have the bandwidth to seriously consider it—not just yet.

"You can deal with only one milestone at a time when you have a child on the spectrum," she says. "We already had all these people working with us on Luv, Michael. We had all these orders, and the business came with all these challenges, and I just couldn't think about all the challenges still to come. Where Michael might live in the future, whether or not he'd be able to live on his own—these things seemed like something I didn't have to worry about for another ten years. He wasn't there yet on his journey. *We* weren't there yet."

Trouble was, Michael was on a whole other timetable. And his journey soon took him in a whole other direction. Sadly, and perhaps inevitably, he started having some behavioral issues. He was acting up, acting erratically—a pattern of behavior, it turns out, that is not at all uncommon among young men with autism, who sometimes go through hormonal and other changes in their late teens that dramatically alter their behavior. In Michael's case, this meant that he often became agitated. He was injuring himself, was combative around other people, and was so totally not like himself. Michael had never been prone to these types of outbursts and had never been on any medication to quiet his behavior. His parents didn't know how to help him or where to turn, so they scrambled to get the support he needed, the medication he needed.

Curiously, Michael's troubles seemed to dissipate when he was at church with his family. Whatever Lisa and her husband were feeling as they joined their community in song and prayer, Michael was feeling too . . . in his own way. Lisa remembers that there was something about the routine, the familiarity, the connection Michael had always felt with his brother that calmed his erratic behavior. At times, Lisa could look over at Michael during a service and soothe herself into thinking he was just like any of the other young-adult children in attendance. And for the moment, *in* the moment, lost in the rhythms of prayer and ritual, he was. The trouble, though, was that the Dormition of the Virgin Mary Greek Orthodox Church of the Hamptons on Long Island, where Lisa and Dimitri worshiped most Sundays, was in a beach community where the family had a second home, a couple of hours from where they lived full-time, so they couldn't always be present in ways that would have been especially meaningful as Michael struggled.

As Lisa remembers it, Michael's turbulent period lasted nearly two years—one of those challenges his parents didn't see coming. In that time, he had to stop working at Luv, Michael, and Lisa and Dimitri were pushed to accept a placement for him in what was known as a crisis home—a small group home for only four residents, with a one-to-one staff ratio, in a town about an hour from their home. It was a blessing, but Lisa didn't see it as a blessing at the time.

"That spot became available for Michael and we took it because we felt we had no choice," she recalls. "We were exhausted. We were frightened. We were losing our support staff. Nobody could stay with Michael by themselves. It was really bad. So this was our only option. We didn't even have time to discuss it as a family or to get Michael used to the idea. It all happened so fast."

The way this type of crisis home operates in New York is that it's essentially funded by the state. It's considered a certified placement—all of the benefits Michael was entitled to, from Medicaid to Social Security, were directed to pay for his care. He was turning twenty-one just as the spot in the home became available, so there was nothing his parents had to pay for, but Lisa knew this wasn't a "forever" placement. It was meant to be a stopgap. When the crisis abated and Michael adjusted to his new medications, Lisa would still have to find an appropriate group home where he might live on a permanent basis, so she started looking. It turned out, she wasn't thrilled with the homes she visited. Either there were too many people living in the home, or the staff didn't seem engaged, or the homes were in disrepair. Then she looked at the idea of purchasing a suitable home and donating it to one of the Long Island agencies providing care for the autism community, but under this model the state couldn't guarantee that Michael would even get a bed in the home once it was all set up.

Finally, she remembered the conversation she'd had with the gentleman with a nephew on the spectrum who was developing a group home in partnership with an area church, back when she and Dimitri hadn't been ready to consider such a placement for Michael. She started investigating a self-directed model, pooling state money that might be available to each potential resident and collaborating with other families in a public-private partnership. She especially loved the idea of aligning with her own church, so she reached out to the leadership at the Greek Orthodox church she belonged to in Southampton, where she and Dimitri were thinking of retiring someday.

"They didn't really know what they were saying yes to," she allows, "but they knew they were saying yes to me and to my family, and to this concept of helping families in need."

This last was key, because I've found that the biggest leap in almost any group undertaking is making that first ask.

As it turned out, that big leap wasn't quite so big after all, because one thing I've learned about Lisa Liberatore is that she can be *very* persuasive, especially when it comes to advocating for the needs of her son. After making her pitch to Father Alex at the church and securing his vaguely delineated support, she formed US Autism Homes—a nonprofit network of group homes established for young adults with autism. Soon she found a home within walking distance of the church and started renovating it while Michael was still residing in the crisis home. Luv, Michael was going great guns, but Michael himself hadn't been working in the kitchen since he started having behavioral issues. The business had quickly grown to include nearly thirty participants, employees and interns, and had recently moved into its own commercial kitchen space in the Manhattan neighborhood of Tribeca. The sad irony here was that this had been an initiative to ensure that Michael would have a place to work, a place to put his energy and focus, a place to experience those all-important points of connection outside a school setting, but he just wasn't ready to be in that environment. Instead, he participated in what Lisa describes as a disappointing day-hab program through his crisis-home placement, where there wasn't a whole lot for him to do except sit on a couch in the common room.

"He was just sitting there, rocking," Lisa says. "It was heartbreaking."

Once again, Michael's mom looked to be the change her son needed, so she accelerated the renovations on the group home and went back to Father Alex to see about jump-starting some type of program for Michael and some of the other young adults from his day-hab facility. Father Alex was open to Lisa's ideas—and Lisa, for her part, was open to what Father Alex had to say about the strengths of their community, introducing her to some of the social programming that was already in place at the church that might provide a good fit for Lisa's young-adult charges, as well as to congregants with particular areas of expertise who might be willing to collaborate on some new programming ideas.

The call to *be the change you want to see* is everywhere apparent in the stories I'm sharing in these pages, and here in Lisa Liberatore's story we see it on full display, as she and her husband realized that the best way to help their son Michael was to tap their own strengths and the resources that were already available to them. All of us—in our own lives, in our own ways—are blessed with the ability to do our own version of the same, and a good place to start in on this is to take an accounting of our own assets and line them up in such a way that they might help us to achieve our goals.

As the program got underway, Lisa's initial focus was on cooking—something Michael loved, and something Lisa believed was a suitable, adaptable activity for her son's cohort. It was also an interest that aligned with what the church had to offer. They had a spacious industrial kitchen and a great many congregants who were already working as volunteer chefs and servers for church functions. She recruited nine people from Michael's day-hab for weekly cooking sessions at the church. Father Alex opened up the church kitchen for their use, while Lisa hired a teacher to give food-safety lessons. When the young chefs were ready, they helped prepare the traditional Greek items that were typically served at church events: spinach pies, grape leaves, cookies.

This went on for about a year, until the renovations on the group home were complete.

About those renovations: Lisa added two bedrooms to the three-bedroom house. All of the bedrooms were on the main level. Then she worked with her architect to dig a new basement to accommodate a gym and a home theater. On the second level, she designed a common room, where the residents could hang out and play video games and take Zoom classes. At the same time, she was figuring out her staffing and programming needs. Her priority, though, was to fill the beds, because of course their group home could not be a group home without a group, and here one of Lisa's first calls was to her sister, whose son Christian was also on the autism spectrum. Christian was about three years older than his cousin Michael, and very different. He was much more verbal, much more social. Still, the two boys were close, and Lisa knew it would be an easier transition for each of them if they entered into this new situation together.

At the time, Lisa's sister wasn't quite ready to consider a group home environment for Christian, but when Lisa explained that she couldn't hold a bed for her nephew indefinitely, she reconsidered, and the two cousins moved into the house in June 2020. It was the height of the COVID pandemic, so staffing and programming were limited at the outset. Lisa had recruited a young man from Nigeria who had been working in the church's youth ministry the previous summer to run the house and act as a kind of head counselor; she was able to arrange for him to stay on in the United States following his divinity studies with a clinical pastoral care visa. He became US Autism Homes' first hire.

Soon, as COVID restrictions eased and word spread throughout Long Island's autism community, Lisa began hearing from other parents with adult children on the spectrum who thought this unique group home setup might be an appropriate fit for their sons as well. Eventually, two other young men, Dimitri and Eric, joined the group—on a transitional basis at first. They started visiting the house several days a week and participating in the classes and activities Lisa was organizing before moving into the house full-time in the fall of 2021. By this point, the alliance with the Greek Orthodox church was taking full and formidable shape. Lisa's vague ask had become way more specific, and Father Alex and others in leadership positions at the church were extremely accommodating and open to the ideas brought to them by Lisa and the other parents.

Most significantly, the group had been given a designated

classroom at the church, and it was in almost constant use. Lisa hired an art teacher, a drum teacher, a yoga teacher. If one of the residents expressed a particular interest, she brought in a teacher from the community—usually a congregant with an expertise in a certain area looking to volunteer his or her time. She hired a special-ed teacher to come in twice a week to run a program called Transitioning to Adulthood, in which the residents were taught essential life skills such as cleaning, budgeting, and scheduling.

Cut to today and US Autism Homes now operates four group homes on the East End of Long Island—two homes for young women and two for young men, all within just a few minutes of each other, and all just a short walk to Lisa's church, where residents participate in church activities and benefit from the many classes and programs put in place by Lisa and her staff. When looking for properties to develop for the program, Lisa considered proximity to the church as her number one priority, because she knew how necessary it was to provide these residents with a lifeline to the world around, and to each other.

Meanwhile, Luv, Michael continues to operate as a stand-alone affiliated business, helping to bring awareness to the group home movement spearheaded by Lisa and her husband, and to support programs and services for the local autistic community.

(By the way, their granola is delicious!)

Happily, mercifully, the church was able to stay open during the COVID lockdown of 2020—in a safe way. Church leadership installed an HVAC system to clear and circulate the air and put mindful protocols in place requiring masks and social distancing. And in the goes-without-saying department, I should mention that all the group home residents attend services every Sunday, to worship in their own ways. One of the residents is Jewish, another is Catholic, and several come from home environments where they were never exposed to organized religion.

One of her particular joys, Lisa says, is seeing her son Michael thrive in a church setting—just as he had once done as a young boy, emulating his older brother as an altar server, only now he is there on his own terms, worshiping in his own way, with housemates and friends who are committed as much to each other as to their church community.

"We might be affiliated with a Greek Orthodox church, but we want all of our residents to feel welcome," Lisa explains. "We don't want anyone thinking we're pushing a religious agenda. We're completely nondenominational, but what we're finding is that our group really enjoys the experience of being in church together. Our families are all okay with this. It's one of the things we make sure about before we bring in a new resident. Remember, the intention here is to create a forever home for the individual. We're not looking for a short-term solution to someone's home situation, or to provide a transitional independent-living situation as these kids age out of their own environments and their parents are no longer able to care for them. No, this is meant to be a living, breathing, sustainable thing, a way to build a life, and for my husband and me, our religious community has always been a part of that. For Michael and his brother, too.

"And if it works out that the young men and women we serve are inspired to live a life of faith, through our church, or any other church, then that is a whole other blessing."

Indeed—a blessing inside of a blessing.

CHAPTER 5

BOB FREEMAN

Have a Little Interfaith

This story found me in the unlikeliest place, in the unlikeliest way—but I guess this is only fitting because it's just about the unlikeliest story you're likely to come across regarding the establishment and practice of organized religion. Unlikely or not, it's the kind of story that shines a light on the very best of us and signals what it means to be a person of faith—and, as important, what can happen when that faith is lit by an impossible dream that in the end turns out to be not so impossible after all.

What I especially love about this story is that it offers a beautiful reminder that we are all here on this earth together, joined not by our shared faith so much as by our shared humanity. We each pray in our own ways, or not at all, but no matter what we believe, we must remain steadfast in our belief in each other. We must find a way to work with each other, to talk to each other, to coexist with each other, and in these challenging times, with the war in Israel and the tensions dividing our Muslim and Jewish communities, this has never been more apparent—or important.

Here's the story behind the story: I was in Las Vegas, for one of the inaugural shows at a spectacular new concert venue called Sphere, where the Irish rock band U2 was in the middle of a months-long residency. I'd known the band's lead singer, Bono, for more than twenty years, going back to when I was a member of Congress and he came to Washington to discuss world debt relief. Out of that first meeting, I was honored to lead the floor fight to grow a $60 million debt-relief effort to more than $435 million for African debt relief. And out of *that* I met Bobby Shriver, the oldest child of Sargent Shriver and Eunice Kennedy Shriver.

Bobby was Bono's guy on Capitol Hill, but he'd been a journalist before going to law school and becoming an advocate for global change. He'd helped to start the ONE Campaign to fight AIDS and extreme poverty in Africa, and an organization called DATA (which stands for Debt, AIDS, Trade, Africa)—two dovetailing efforts that led to the establishment of (RED), which was launched in 2006 and has since generated more than $750 million for the Global Fund, one of the world's largest funders of global health initiatives, through brand partnerships with American Express, Apple, Microsoft, Dell, and other leading companies.

He struck me, then and still, as an incredible guy—a real *doer*—and over the years he's become a good and trusted friend. As you might imagine with that kind of track record, Bobby Shriver could be a pretty persuasive guy, and here he persuaded me to join him in Vegas for this concert. That's how it worked out that Bobby and I were hanging out at the afterparty, comparing notes, taking in the scene, when I started telling him about this book. Back then, it was just an idea I had, to shine a light on some of the extraordinary work being done by ordinary individuals out to make our world a better place under the auspices of their faith-based institutions and organizations, and while that idea took shape, I was determined to cast a wide net looking for stories I might include in the mix. This was my standard operating mode as I was getting this book off the ground, because I've found that word of mouth is often the best way to learn what's going on around the country— the original "Google search," in my estimation—so I was corralling everyone I knew who might be in a position to turn me on to a compelling story.

Bobby introduced me to his friend Susie Buffett, the daughter of Warren and Susan Buffett. Susie is one of the world's great philanthropists, with a focus on public education, human services, child welfare, and social justice issues. I told her, too, about the idea for this book, because it didn't matter to me whether I'd known you for twenty years or twenty minutes if I thought you might be in a position to help me solve this particular puzzle, and it got her thinking.

"You should talk to Bob Freeman," she said, as if this went without saying.

"Okay," I said. "Who's Bob Freeman?"

Susie told me briefly about Bob and the development of the Tri-Faith Center in Omaha, Nebraska, home to three distinct houses of worship representing Jews, Christians, and Muslims. The places of worship are all built on a beautiful thirty-eight-acre integrated campus in Omaha and are connected by an interfaith center at the heart of the complex. Leadership from Temple Israel, Countryside Community Church, and the American Muslim Institute offer programming and youth activities designed to bring the three communities together in fellowship and joint opportunities for service and worship.

Now, on its face, the idea of a multifaith approach to organized religion was fantastic and thrilling and altogether remarkable, but to hear of it in this setting, at a concert led by one of the world's great ambassadors, in this otherworldly venue that was also pretty fantastic and thrilling and altogether remarkable, made it especially so, and I thanked Susie for the tip and asked whether she would make an introduction.

Soon after, she did—and now here I am, all this time later, introducing Bob Freeman in these pages. His is a story I didn't know I needed to tell when I started in on this project, but it's one that has come to epitomize the very many stories I'm out to share. And one that reminds us of the power to be found in dreaming big and pushing the envelope and refusing to take no for an answer.

Officially, the Tri-Faith Initiative was completed in August 2020, at the height of the pandemic, when the final building on the campus was completed—the interfaith center that sits at the heart of the complex. You'd think that an ambitious religious complex such as this one, joining followers of the world's three major Abrahamic religions, not just in proximity but in community and fellowship, would capture the world's attention, but outside Nebraska it didn't exactly dominate the news cycle. I think one of the reasons the dedication of the center went largely unnoticed was that the world had gone dark, and a great many folks had turned their attention inward, keeping to themselves until there was some clarity on how the COVID virus was spread and on how it might be vaccinated against and treated.

Unofficially, work on the Tri-Faith Center had begun more than fifteen years earlier, when the world was in an entirely different place, with a series of pie-in-the-sky conversations jump-started by Bob Freeman, who for several years had served as the president of Omaha's Temple Israel congregation and who continued to be active in synagogue leadership as this complicated partnership got off the ground.

Actually, it started with a dream—a specific dream Bob had on the night of September 17, 2005. (He remembers the date as if it were yesterday, he says.) I'll tell you about that dream in a beat, but before I get to it, I need to let you know what was going on with Bob and his cherished temple community in the years leading up to it. At the time, Temple Israel was experiencing some growing pains— the congregation, a reform community that now serves more than seven hundred families, was bursting at the seams in its original building, which each year was in more and more disrepair and less and less able to accommodate its expanding membership. The congregation was torn between looking to build a new synagogue on the west side of town, where most of Omaha's Jewish population tended to reside, or renovating the current building, which would have allowed them to remain at their present location for the next long while.

As it happened, Bob wasn't in favor of relocating the temple, although his preference was entirely personal: He lived just a few blocks from the current location and loved that he was able to walk to services. Still, he recognized that as the city's Jewish population moved west and younger synagogue members were more likely to be living in neighborhoods across town, he had no choice but to help with the relocation effort. Understand, Bob's "help" went beyond a simple endorsement of the idea to build a new synagogue across town. Since he was a former synagogue president, his voice carried a lot of weight in the community. He was also the temple's lawyer, with expertise in business, corporate, and real estate law, so he had a lot to offer here, and beginning in 2003 he joined the effort to find a new site in West Omaha.

For years Bob and his cohort on Temple Israel's search committee looked for an appropriate location, but the properties they found were either too big, too small, too expensive, or otherwise unsuitable. You know how it is when you're out looking for the perfect house or the perfect parcel of land. You find yourself scouring every listing, knowing that when the right opportunity comes along, you'll have to jump on it. That's what was going on here, only the right opportunity never seemed to materialize, and after a couple of years Bob and his group were beginning to wonder whether the stars would ever align and lead them to a new site.

This was right about the time Bob had that dream.

"I'm not someone who dreams a lot," he says now, as a caveat. "And I'm not someone who believes in God-given inspiration. I'm a very practical, very pragmatic person, and anyone who knows me would confirm that I'm not a dreamer. But there is no question that, on this night, I had this dream. This unusually long and extremely detailed dream. It was all so clear, and I can't think of any explanation for it other than that this was God's way of intervening and putting a bunch of thoughts into my head, for whatever reason, because I woke up early that Saturday morning, which I often do, and grabbed a legal pad, which I also often do. I have always kept legal pads around the house, so I was in the habit of writing stuff down and organizing my thoughts in this way. I started writing furiously and filling all these pages. Nothing like this had ever happened to me before, and I didn't want to forget anything, so I set it all down."

After a while, Bob looked up from this frenzy of writing and gathering his thoughts and realized he should probably go outside for a walk to clear his head. He took his legal pad with him, though, because he wasn't done taking notes. He must have been quite a sight as he roamed the streets of Omaha with pad in hand, stopping here and there to write for another few moments, then continuing on—Bob's old-school version of texting while driving, I guess.

At one point he found himself in front of a favorite coffee shop in his neighborhood, about a mile from his house, so he ducked in for a cup of coffee just as the place was opening up for the day, taking another few moments to write down another few thoughts before continuing on his walk.

By now it was about seven thirty in the morning and Bob had been at it for a couple of hours. As he continued to think through the stuff of his dream, he realized he was wandering past the driveway to the temple parking lot. He hadn't been paying attention to where he was headed, but the temple had been in his thoughts all morning, so he remembers thinking it was only fitting that he was drawn to it, with or without a conscious thought.

What's also fitting is that Bob arrived at the Temple Israel driveway that morning at the same time as the temple's senior rabbi, Rabbi Aryeh Azriel, who was also Bob's good friend. The two men had kids the same age and had traveled together and spent a lot of time working side by side during Bob's term as synagogue president, then while Bob served as legal counsel for the temple. They had a familiar way about them, Bob recalls, an ease in communicating, that on this early morning was on full display in the temple parking lot, as neither one of them could figure out what the other one was doing there at that early hour.

Bob couldn't imagine why the rabbi was driving onto the temple grounds a couple of hours before he had to lead services that morning, while the rabbi wondered why his friend seemed to be pacing back and forth nursing a cup of coffee and writing determinedly on a legal pad.

"What's up?" Rabbi Azriel asked, after he'd pulled into his parking spot. "Why are you standing in our driveway, writing stuff down on a legal pad at seven thirty in the morning?"

Bob wasn't ready to share the details of his dream just yet. He had nothing to hide, but at the same time there was nothing to tell. "I can't say," he said.

"You can tell me anything, Bob," the rabbi said. "Matter of fact, you already *do*."

This was true. The two men spoke often on matters of faith, synagogue business, family issues, politics, and the news of the day. But this was different, Bob thought. This was wild, and out there. Certainly, it went way beyond anything the two men had talked about in their previous conversations. What he had to share, what had been on his mind as he awakened from his dream this morning, was big. Too big for him to just blurt out, because the vision that had come to him in his dream was so immense in its scope and in its possibilities, so untethered to everything he understood about religion and practicality, that he didn't want even his good friend the rabbi to dismiss it out of hand.

He needed to think it all the way through before giving it voice.

"Look," Bob finally said, after a long pause. "I'm having some big thoughts. I had a dream last night. I've been working all morning, writing, thinking what it all might mean. It definitely involves you and the temple, but I need a little more time to pull it all together."

Rabbi Azriel said, "Take all the time you need, Bob. But now I'm curious. I need to hear what's got you so excited."

"I promise," Bob assured. "You'll be the first person I talk to about it, but first I want to make sure I'm ready to talk about it."

And so the two men wished each other a good Shabbos and continued on their separate ways.

A dozen or so legal-pad pages and a couple of days later, Bob had fleshed out the bit of idea that had come to him in his dream—an idea to build an entirely new synagogue building, next door to an entirely new church, next door to an entirely new mosque, on a centrally located parcel of land big enough to accommodate the needs of these three disparate, sometimes conflicting communities, together with a dynamic interfaith center at the heart of the property tying the whole wondrous compound together.

An impossible dream, most people might think. But Bob Freeman was not one of those people.

Before calling the rabbi, Bob sketched out a chart and worked up a formal pitch to make sure his idea came across in the best possible light. Then he set up a meeting for later on that week, and as he went to the synagogue to keep the appointment, his mind raced with this vision. He sat down in the rabbi's office at the appointed time and went right into his pitch, only he doesn't remember sitting all that much. He was too excited to sit. And he couldn't get the words out fast enough.

When he was through, the rabbi looked at him and said, "Wow. I agree. Let's do it."

"He bought it immediately," Bob remembers. "I think I knew he would, but I wanted to be sure. He's really involved in a lot of interfaith things. He doesn't think anybody has a monopoly on the right religion or the right way to find God. As Jews, we have our own path, and that's fine. But Christians, they've got their own path, too. And Muslims, same deal. Rabbi Azriel was never about trying to convert the world to his way of thinking. He was much more of a bridge builder."

To illustrate the rabbi's bridge-building tendencies, Bob told me about the time right after September 11 when Rabbi Azriel recruited a group of synagogue members and area Jewish leaders to watch over Omaha's small but growing Muslim community, which had just rented a small building downtown to use as a prayer space and for gatherings. Compellingly, the rabbi led the effort to stand in solidarity with his Muslim neighbors, organizing volunteers in shifts to remain on-site at the makeshift mosque for the next days and weeks to make sure nobody vandalized the property or threatened any members of that community.

As a practical matter, the rabbi's enthusiasm went only so far. There was still the matter of winning the support of Temple Israel leadership—and, after clearing *that* hurdle, bringing in local Christian and Muslim leaders to talk through the concept and see how it might fit with their own visions.

Bob took his pitch to the synagogue board, but after having been on the receiving end of Rabbi Azriel's wild enthusiasm for the plan, he was a little discouraged to get back only mild enthusiasm from the friends and fellow congregants he'd worked alongside for the past many years.

"Basically, what they said was 'Freeman, these are a lot of big ideas and they're great, but they're a little far-fetched,'" Bob recounts. "And I understood that response, of course. I think I even anticipated it. I mean, as far as I could tell, something like this has never been done before in the history of the world. In fact, there isn't a church, a synagogue, and a mosque that have been *accidentally* built right next to each other, let alone on purpose."

And so Bob went back to his legal pads and noodled with the idea some more. With a thing like this, he was realizing, there had to be a reason it had never happened organically, even in our densely populated urban areas where Jews and Christians and Muslims lived and worked close to each other, along with members of other faith communities. That reason, he concluded, was the fact that nobody had ever tried to make something like this happen.

He was out to change that.

The Temple Israel board was willing to get behind the idea, but no one was confident that he could pull it off. In fact, nobody thought it was likely to happen. But because Bob was such an active and respected member of the community, and because he already had the support of the rabbi, they agreed to let him pursue the matter on the temple's behalf.

To hear Bob tell it, it's almost as though his friends and fellow congregants indulged him on this wild notion, primarily because he had earned their respect and goodwill over the years, and only a little bit because they actually thought it was a viable prospect.

"They told me to go out and talk to people," Bob recalls, "so I guess you could say I was deputized to look into all of this. But they also told me that what they really wanted from me was my support for building a new synagogue in the western part of the city."

Now, there are a lot of moving parts to this story, which makes sense because the Tri-Faith complex took nearly fifteen years to complete. Fifteen years! Bob could write a whole book about it—and I suspect he will, someday. But for now, for *this* book, where Bob's story is sharing space with all of these other wonderful stories, I'll need to cut to the chase. The long-story-short version of what happened next is that Bob got together with Rabbi Azriel and started reaching out to Omaha's religious leaders hoping to develop some traction for this idea.

Over time, they did.

The great lesson here? To keep at it. No matter what. No matter how far-fetched or unlikely your mission. If you believe in it, trust that you have the power to make it so—or, at least, that you have the power to convince a group of caring, thinking souls to throw in with you on whatever it is you're pursuing and help turn your lone voice into a resounding chorus that cannot be ignored. Even if it takes fifteen years!

Probably my favorite story Bob shared for this book was a memory of his first formal meeting with five members of a local Muslim delegation. The meeting was held at the local library in February 2006, about five months after Bob's game-changing dream. Before he left for the library, Bob's wife gave him a dish of food she'd prepared for him to share with the other men at the meeting. The rabbi's wife also sent something. The two friends couldn't understand why they needed to "cater" this gathering, but they knew not to question their wives, and when they arrived at the library, they were happily surprised to discover that four members of the Muslim delegation had also brought plates of food, prepared by *their* wives.

"Apparently, you need to have food to share at something like this," Bob considers. "You can't just talk. You have to eat."

Out of that meeting, Bob prepared a memo of understanding setting out the plans and principles that had been discussed and outlining a path forward. The memo stressed that each group would operate autonomously—the Jews would purchase their own land, raise their own money, build their own temple, do their own thing. The Muslims would purchase their own land, raise their own money, build their own mosque, do their own thing. They had yet to reach out to a Christian coalition to bring them in on the deal, but the same terms would apply. The only partnership at this early stage, binding one group to another, was a commitment to seek a centrally located parcel of land big enough to accommodate all three structures, with the possibility of a shared parking lot and the prospect of a unified design.

"Oh, and one more thing," Bob adds. "If we ended up doing this, we wanted to set aside three acres in the middle and raise another couple million to build an interfaith center, but if that didn't work out, or if the money ran out and we could only afford to put a picnic table in the middle at that point, that'd be great, too. We could meet there and have a cup of coffee and talk to each other."

Another favorite story: Early on in the planning, in the fall of 2005, U2 was scheduled to perform at the Qwest Center in Omaha. Bob had been instrumental in helping to build the arena just a couple of years earlier, so he had a rooting interest in seeing these big acts when they came to town. And, serendipitously, Susie

Buffett was on hand because she's a huge fan, so the moment ties in to how I'd connected with Bob for this book, but the reason this concert rates a mention in this account is that during the concert Bono seemed to speak directly into this mission from the stage. Bob remembers standing with Susie B., as he calls her, and marveling at Bono's peaceful, hope-filled message of unity and inclusion—a message Bob believes was meant to underline his own peaceful, hope-filled quest to join *all* of Omaha's children of Abraham in worship and community.

"I still hadn't told a lot of people what we were up to," Bob tells, "and Bono steps to the mic between songs and starts talking about people getting along. People from all religions, all backgrounds, all walks of life. It was amazing, the way he was talking about the very same things *we* were talking about, only he was doing it in front of seventeen thousand people. Right here in Omaha, where we were looking to bring all these communities together. So, yeah, I took it as a sign."

After the concert, he sent a cryptic note to Susie Buffett telling her about his dream, his meetings with the Muslims, and the synchronicity of hearing these words of unity from the concert stage, but she had no idea what he was talking about.

"She thought I was nuts," he reports.

Nuts or not, he kept at it.

With a commitment from the Muslim delegation to pursue the matter on principle, Bob turned his attention to finding a church to share in his vision. His thinking at the time was that, since Omaha's Christian population was largely Catholic, they would wind up partnering with a Catholic church, so the first call he made was to the archbishop. He introduced himself, shared what he was up to, and asked for a meeting. Bob showed up at the archbishop's office with the rabbi and the lead member of the Muslim delegation, Dr. Syed Mohiuddin, the chief of cardiology and director of the Cardiac Center at Creighton University's School of Medicine, who would go on to become a founding member of the American Muslim Institute.

The archbishop invited some of his senior priests and advisers to attend the meeting, and when everyone was seated, he kicked things off by talking about the state of the Catholic Church in Omaha, the growth the church was expecting in the years ahead, the new initiatives being undertaken at home and abroad. He went on and on, according to Bob, knowing full well that these men had come to discuss the building of a new church as part of an inter- faith effort but avoiding the subject entirely.

"We haven't even said a word," Bob says, "and he's just talking about anything and everything but what we're all there to discuss, and then he's done. I was stunned. I just said, 'Your Excellency, we have these ideas, and we'd like to talk about them with you.' But he wouldn't let me finish. He waved his hands and said, 'No, no, no. We are not interested in doing anything like that.'"

Frustrated, Bob and his group realized they would have to look elsewhere for church participation, but then a remarkable thing happened—or, at least, a remarkable thing *nearly* happened. A very nearly remarkable thing that confirmed for Bob Freeman that he was on the right path with this tri-faith idea, even though it didn't exactly move this conversation forward.

Here's what happened: The archbishop, still holding court, started talking about the election of Pope Benedict XVI and the recent release of his first-ever writings as pope, which the arch- bishop had stayed up all night reading.

"I didn't want to hear about the new pope and his writings," Bob says. "I was there to talk about the building of an interfaith campus, but finally the archbishop finishes whatever he's saying about Pope Benedict, and the rabbi stands and shares that he had also been up the night before reading the new pope's writings. I'm thinking, *This is unbelievable*. I'm thinking, *This is another sign*, because Rabbi Azriel is telling the archbishop what he learned from the pope as a Jew leading a Reform Jewish community here in America. It was quite something, but what happened next was a real showstopper."

Here's what happened next: Dr. Mohiuddin rose and announced that he, too, had read the pope's writings, and he proceeded to share what he had learned as a Muslim man in Omaha, Nebraska.

Pretty remarkable, don't you think?

"The hair on the back of my neck is standing up straight," Bob recalls. "I'm the last guy who'd stay up late reading the pope's writings, but I'm in a room with a Catholic and a Jew and a Muslim who are sharing this same experience, and I'm thinking this couldn't be happening anywhere else in America, maybe even anywhere else in the world. And I allow myself to think, of the archbishop, that surely he can't participate in a conversation such as this one, experiencing this kind of connection with a Jew and a Muslim, and still hold to his view that the church had no interest in something like this. I mean, he *had* to see there was something going on here, right?"

Well . . . not so fast. The archbishop wasn't moving from his place of disinterest, and Bob and his group were shown the door, and as they left, the three men looked at each other in disbelief. And frustration. And wonder.

"On the one hand, it was a terrible outcome," Bob explains. "But on the other hand, there was this miracle that happened, with the way everyone came together over the new pope and his writings. What was clear, though, was that we weren't going to get anywhere with the Catholics, and that if we were going to find Christian participation, we would have to keep looking."

For the next long while, Bob's cobbled-together religious consortium looked as though it would include an Episcopal church. Not incidentally, Bob's wife had been raised Episcopalian, and Bob had gone to church with his wife many times over the years before they decided to raise their children in the Jewish tradition, so he felt a special connection to the denomination. But when the Episcopal

Diocese of Nebraska couldn't decide which of their up-and-running congregations it would recommend moving to a proposed new site, they backed out of the deal. The group ended up partnering with Countryside Community Church, under the leadership of Reverend Eric Elnes, which was part of the United Church of Christ.

With religious partners in place, Bob allowed himself to start thinking that this crazy idea he'd had one night might actually become a reality. Trouble was, his group still hadn't been able to find an appropriate parcel of land. They got close a couple of times, but the deals always fell apart for one reason or another. And then the group heard that a local golf course was closing its doors. Like a lot of golf courses after the stock market crash of 2008, the Island Country Club was struggling. They'd undertaken a couple of big-capital projects just a couple of years earlier, including the building of a new clubhouse, but now they couldn't afford to make their payments because they were losing members.

With the golf course property apparently in play, the real estate team that had been assembled to steer the tri-faith development effort looked on with great interest. The course was located in the middle of West Omaha, on a busy street, less than a half mile off the highway. The location seemed perfect, but Bob was bothered by the fact that the club had been predominantly Jewish—at one time, half of its members were Temple Israel congregants—and he didn't like the optics of a temple putting a Jewish country club out of business by negotiating to buy their land, so he got with his group and decided they could pursue this land opportunity only if the property went into foreclosure.

When that happened, however, the tri-faith consortium was outbid by a group of real estate developers who were looking to build a multiuse facility with private homes, shopping centers, and offices.

"We were disappointed, of course," Bob reflects, "but I knew from all the real estate deals that I'd done that the developers needed to set aside a certain percentage of their land for public use. It could be for a church, or a park, or a community center, or whatever. I approached the buyers right there at the sale. I introduced myself and told them what we were looking to do, and offered to buy about twenty-five percent of the land they'd just purchased, at fair market value, which would at the same time solve the civic-development problem they would be facing down the road.

"Well, these guys also thought I was nuts," he continues. "I mean, a synagogue, a church, and a mosque, throwing in together like this? It was the most far-fetched thing they could imagine. But they also knew that our group had done some major real estate development work in Omaha, and that we knew what we were talking about, so we set up a meeting."

In the end, the interfaith group came to terms with the real estate developers and purchased the necessary land, in four separate transactions. The temple purchased approximately fourteen acres. The church purchased about eight acres. The mosque required roughly six acres. And the interfaith center, operating as its own entity, took just over three acres.

In August 2013, Temple Israel completed construction on its new synagogue.

In May 2017, the American Institute of Islamic Studies and Culture (now known as the American Muslim Institute) finished work on its mosque and educational center—a first-of-its-kind facility in Nebraska, by the way.

In April 2019, Countryside Community Church opened its doors.

And, in October 2020, Tri-Faith Initiative, Temple Israel, Countryside Community Church, and the American Muslim Institute celebrated the opening of the Tri-Faith Center, calling it "a beacon of hope and safe haven for dialogue and friendship-building."

One of the signature programs offered by the Tri-Faith Center is its Coffee on the Commons initiative, inviting members of all three congregations, and anyone else in the wider community, to gather for a cup of coffee and informal conversation in the shadow of these three majestic buildings, representing these three majestic faiths. There is no set agenda, no communal call to prayer. There is just coffee and conversation—pretty much how Bob Freeman envisioned it when he first woke from his extraordinary dream.

One of the other great outgrowths is the way the children of these three congregations often engage in interfaith programming, or play together on the center's grounds, growing up beneath the beautiful notion that this is how it is with children all over the world.

These days Bob can often be found walking the grounds of this old golf course reflecting on this unique and rather extraordinary tri-faith community he pretty much dreamed into existence. One of his favorite things to do when he visits, he says, is to seek out a special corner of the interfaith center that he had the architects design into the building. There, he wanders into a small wing at the end of one hallway, where picture windows look out across a creek to the temple and, in the other direction, to the church and the mosque.

"As you stand there," he says, "you can see all three buildings, and I'm not a very religious guy, but without fail, whenever I am at our Tri-Faith Center, I'll spend a few moments in this one spot, and head down the hallway to this little wing, where it's almost like I'm on the bridge of the Starship *Enterprise*, looking out at this wonderful world we've worked so hard to create. We were just a bunch of old farts coming together to solve the needs of our own communities, but at the same time to try something new, and I can look out the windows and see the children. A generation or more of our young people, from all three faiths, growing up together, laughing together, doing community projects together. I can see all three buildings and reflect on what we've accomplished and imagine a world where you can find interfaith communities like this one coexisting all over the country, all over the world.

"It's something to think about."

Yes, it is—even better, it is something to dream about.

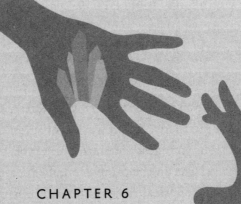

CHAPTER 6

SISTER JOAN DAWBER

Shelter from the Storm

I want to give a shout-out to my wife, Karen, for this one.

As Ohio's first lady, Karen was involved in dozens of initiatives concerning our youngest and most vulnerable citizens. Her focus at the state level was on the promotion of education and literacy programs, and on physical fitness and wellness programs. The more she studied the issues confronting children and families, the more she became concerned about the problem of human trafficking—a crisis not just in Ohio but around the globe. During my two terms as governor, she started spending a lot of time helping to put a face to the faceless victims of this crisis and using her platform to help break the cycle of abuse for so many young women in our state caught in this terrible swirl.

I asked Karen to help me find a story to bring awareness to this issue that might fit with the premise of this book—individuals making a meaningful difference in their part of the world, with the support of their religious communities—and she introduced me to Sister Joan Dawber, the founder and former executive director of LifeWay Network. Boy, am I glad she did!

LifeWay Network is one of only two New York City–area organizations that provides housing and other essential resources for women who have been the victims of labor or sex trafficking. The work they do is heroic, incredible, and lifesaving. And because of the discreet nature of that work—safeguarding women who flee from their captors—it is often unrecognized.

Early on in my first term as governor, I helped to pass legislation to shield juvenile human-trafficking victims from prostitution charges. The law had been written in such a way that the state could prosecute young victims alongside the traffickers who were forcing them into service, so we were out to change that. The new law also raised the penalties on human traffickers and made it easier for judges to expunge the records of young women with prior solicitation charges.

"Our children need and deserve our protection," I said after House Bill 262, known as the Safe Harbor Law, passed unanimously, calling on the state senate to pass the bill so that we might focus on prosecuting "those guilty of trafficking our kids and support the child-victims who desperately need our help."

Human trafficking, of course, is a modern form of slave trading, and the numbers are alarming. By some accounts it ranks as the fastest-growing criminal enterprise on the planet, with an estimated 40.3 million people currently enslaved around the world—more than there's ever been, at any time in history. Approximately 17,000 foreign nationals are trafficked into the United States each year, and it's been reported that the average age of victims being introduced into the world of sex trafficking in this country is thirteen. Because so many of these (mostly) women are anonymous, it's difficult for experts to calculate the total number of victims currently living in the United States, but it is believed to be in the hundreds of thousands.

To be clear, the human-trafficking crisis isn't limited to immigrants and newly settled women. Victims include vulnerable women and men from all walks of life, in all circumstances, including those struggling with substance abuse and mental-health issues, those living in unstable home or foster-care environments, and on and on. Sister Joan might have been confronting the problem in and around New York City, but trafficking finds its way into many of our cities and suburbs, and into our back yards, all over the country.

The situation is tragic—and, for those looking to make a difference in this area, it is also maddening, because so many of the victims of human trafficking are unable to make themselves known. After all, how can you possibly help to solve a crisis if you don't even know where to begin?

Sister Joan has now retired from her day-to-day role with LifeWay, but when you spend even just a little bit of time talking to her about it, you get the sense that she'll always keep connected to the effort in some way.

How she got it going speaks to the ways many issues advanced by the Catholic Church come to the fore. As many readers might know, Roman Catholic congregations from all over the world gather every four years in Rome to discuss where they might place their emphasis in the years ahead. The Mother General, the Mother Superior, and the congregational leaders come together to address their concerns, and one year several of the African sisters brought the issue of human trafficking to the table. After much discussion it was agreed that the leadership would take this issue back to their congregations and begin to think what they might do to address it at the local level—understanding full well that the women they might eventually serve in this humanitarian way would likely be in hiding or unable to reach out for help, and that those offering assistance could expect to also be at risk.

Now, a proclamation such as this is no small thing, because these conferences represent more than one million sisters, so there's no way to overstate the significance of these gatherings, and when word reached Sister Joan back in New York that she was meant to study this issue, she immediately started praying on it.

"The first I learned about it was through a letter sent to us by our congregational leader," Sister Joan reflects. "In the letter, she said she expected us to learn about the plight of these women and to pray for them, and it greatly affected me. I thought about it a lot. I studied everything I could about the subject, and what I was learning was pretty awful. I must admit, I was somewhat afraid of it."

Sister Joan's fear, she says, had mostly to do with the stories she was reading about it, the ugliness of the stories and the desperation of the young women, but she was also afraid that she didn't have it in her to make a difference on this issue or that it could be meaningfully addressed from her little corner of the world.

Still, she prayed on it some more, and what she discovered through prayer was a way forward.

"This is what I believe," she says. "When you pray, it's not what you are praying for that changes. It's *you* that changes. So I began to think about it more. I began to look into it and read about it more. And I connected with some of the other sisters who were here in New York and we created a coalition against human trafficking."

Out of that coalition of sisters representing seven congregations in the New York metropolitan area there emerged a consensus that the group could indeed do something about this issue, so they set about it. Sister Joan went to her congregation in Richmond Hill, Queens, and arranged for a grant of $30,000 to help get the project off the ground. Her congregation, the Sisters of Charity Halifax, is based in Nova Scotia, but she had always served their community in New York City, and through her research she had determined that there was a pressing need for this type of outreach in the metropolitan area.

This right here is a persuasive reminder of the incremental power just waiting to be tapped in our faith-based institutions. Sometimes that power can be found in a volunteer force of caring individuals who are willing and able to throw in with you to help a thing get done. Sometimes it's the offer of a communal space, as we learned from Lisa Liberatore in a previous chapter, which helped her to launch her great granola initiative with her son Michael in her church's industrial kitchen. And sometimes it comes through much-needed funds, and here I think it helps to note that Sister Joan was careful to key her ask to match the resources of the organization she was soliciting. She knew that if she went to church leadership with a request for funding that was within reach, she would get the money she needed to move this initiative forward.

In addition to the grant, she was able to get the congregation to give over an empty room in one of their buildings for her to use as an office. She had a desk, a chair, and a computer, and that was pretty much it.

"Job one for me was two things," she remembers. "The first was to make sure all the members of this coalition were working in tandem, and the second was to reach out to some of the other congregations in the area to let them know what we were doing."

In this second regard, at least, Sister Joan and her cohort were immediately successful, because they soon grew their coalition—the New York Coalition of Religious Congregations to Stop Trafficking in Persons—to include more than thirty local congregations, but their efforts to identify vulnerable women who might be in need of their services weren't exactly getting them anywhere.

"You have to realize," Sister Joan explains, "this was the early 2000s, and people weren't really talking about human trafficking the way they are today. Even in the social service agencies in the city, they weren't talking about it. There were articles being written about it, but at the same time it was like a secret thing. These days, it's so much more out in the open, and so much more talked about, but back then this wasn't the case."

That all started to change as city agencies began holding open meetings on the issue, where Sister Joan was at last able to identify dozens of survivors of human trafficking in and around the New York City area in desperate need of housing. Thousands of women each year are landing in New York and forced into sexual exploitation or sold into forced labor, and local churches are leading the effort to offer a kind of sanctuary to the few victims with an ability to momentarily break free of their captors.

Troublingly, there wasn't a single designated safehouse in the city where these women could get the health care and job training and psychological support they required to start living independent lives. As a workaround solution, several were being temporarily placed in domestic violence shelters, because their case workers pointed out that they'd been abused by their domestic partners, but those environments were not ideally suited to this population—and the people running those programs weren't exactly enthusiastic about making these shelters a target.

It turned out that Sister Joan's congregation owned a neighborhood property that would soon be empty. The sisters who had been living there were moving out, and the congregation had yet to determine a need for the building going forward, so Sister Joan went to the leadership team to ask them to hold on to the property for the next little while to give her group time to see whether they might turn it into a viable shelter for survivors of human trafficking.

"We had enough funding to go for a year," she recalls. "That was all we could count on, going in, but our thinking at the time was if we go for a year, we can see what happens. You know, if it comes to a close, it comes to a close. But at least we would have tried. And at least we would have offered a temporary haven for some of these women."

That's a powerful lesson, I think, for anyone looking to make a difference. You might have a grand vision in mind of what you'd like to accomplish or how many people you'd like to serve, but you can't always realize that vision right out of the gate. Or maybe you can, but in a way that's not quite so grand. Sometimes you need to move in an incremental way, and if it works out that your vision never comes fully into focus, because it's just not realistic or the timing isn't right or you can't recruit enough people or raise enough money to advance your cause, you can either recalibrate that dream so that it aligns with the reality you're now facing or content yourself with knowing you've given it a shot and helped in some way. We'd all like to be able to make a big difference in whatever it is we set out to do, but sometimes only a small difference is within reach—and those small differences have a way of adding up, believe me.

Back to Sister Joan and LifeWay Network: That first house was able to accommodate seven residents, and Sister Joan knew at the outset that one year might not be long enough to help get these women back on their feet, so she went back to the congregation and made an appeal for additional funding—this time raising more than $300,000 through direct appeals to the participating coalition congregations. Not only that, another house in the Sisters of Charity Halifax real estate portfolio soon became available—this one with room for five additional residents—so the program was up and running in what felt to Sister Joan like no time flat.

It was around this time that Sister Joan realized she needed to come up with a name for this initiative. She was working with a lawyer trying to formally establish her effort, and just before she needed to file her incorporation papers, she made a final trip to the computer in search of inspiration. "I kept coming back to the word *Life*," she reflects, "which always speaks to me in the person of Jesus Christ. Life, with a capital *L*, is Jesus. And then I thought of the word *Way*, and its many meanings, but here again, for me, with a capital *W*, it signals the way of Jesus in the world, and of course it reminds us that before we called our faith Christianity, it was called 'the Way.' So I loved the message of those two words together. And then, of course, because we had so many congregations working with us on this through our coalition, I wanted to tie everybody in, so we became LifeWay Network."

The network was formally established in 2007, with the opening of those first two safe houses. (The specific locations of the houses are a closely guarded secret, because many of the women in residence are still being sought by their former captors.) For her efforts in getting LifeWay Network going, Sister Joan was awarded the prestigious Caritas Medal by St. John's University, and she was presented the Sister Christine Mulready Peacemaker Award by Pax Christi Metro New York. But Sister Joan didn't dedicate her life to this mission to win a plaque or earn a citation. She was in it to make a difference—and she has done just that, helping to provide safe housing and a fresh start for more than 120 women since LifeWay

Network opened its doors. That number includes a handful of women who were housed temporarily in a third LifeWay safe house, sharing space with several sisters in the congregation who lived in the home until a spot became available in one of the long-term care homes. For a time, the network also operated another safe house on Long Island, through another congregation altogether, but that residence has since been closed, and Sister Joan reports that there will be other partnerships and alliances, offering housing and other resources, in LifeWay's future.

"That's been the nature of our work," she reflects. "One door opens and another door closes. It opens. It closes."

That fluid mindset takes us back to Sister Joan's thinking at the front end of this effort, when it appeared she would have only enough money to run the program for a year—reminding us of the importance of adapting your mission and your vision to suit your available resources.

Initially, it was thought that residents would stay only a year in the LifeWay safe houses, perhaps owing in some way to the limited budget when the organization opened its doors. But as they studied the issue and prayed on it, Sister Joan and her team concluded that one year would be sufficient time for participants to receive the job training, medical care, and psychological support they would need to move on with their independent lives. It was a calculation meant to provide a goal for residents, help manage the network's limited resources, and provide opportunities for as many victims as possible. But when the very first resident who moved into the house was getting ready to "graduate" from the program, she didn't think she was ready to face the world on her own—and the LifeWay team could only agree.

"Right away, we started using that one-year mark as a guide," Sister Joan says. "In some cases, residents were able to move on in a shorter time. In others, it took a little bit longer for them to gain the confidence and the inner strength they needed."

One of the great challenges early on was getting the women who signed on to the program to trust in the program. According to Sister Joan, there was often a period of weeks, or even months, before some of them could let down their guards and start to feel safe in this new environment. "Usually, when they came to us, it was at least a month before they would feel comfortable," she says. "Even coming to be with us was terrifying for a lot of them. They couldn't understand why we were being so kind to them. They thought we wanted something from them, because of course up until this time if anyone had showed them a kindness, they would have to do something in exchange for that kindness."

Sister Joan has maintained an ongoing relationship with many of the women who have been through the LifeWay program. She regularly receives holiday cards and letters from several former residents and looks on with pride as she collects news of college graduations, graduate school admissions, and wedding and birth announcements—heart-lifting reminders that there can be hope even in heartbreak.

She finds herself leaning on those reminders as she looks back on what she and the other members of her coalition have built. "It's an important ministry," she says, "and an important mission in our church, and in our congregation, and in our world." What's especially important, she says, is that LifeWay Network has been able to get the word out to so many area women caught in these terrible circumstances.

"That's one of the things we'd hear most often, when these women came to live with us," she reflects. "They say, 'We didn't know there was anybody who cared about us.'"

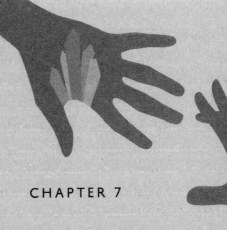

CHAPTER 7

HAL DONALDSON

The Hope Whisperer

I first met Hal Donaldson through my friend Rich Nathan, who for many years served as the senior pastor at Vineyard Columbus—the largest Vineyard church in the world, and the largest church of any denomination in central Ohio. I was governor at the time, and Hal wanted to connect to let me know a little bit about his organization Convoy of Hope, which distributes food, clothing, and other essentials to people in need in the United States and all over the world.

Hal reached out because he was in the business back then of raising awareness for his effort—and he thought that I, as governor, was in a position to help call attention to it. He's still in that business, by the way, which I guess explains how Hal and his team have managed to grow Convoy of Hope into the thirty-fifth largest charity on *Forbes*'s 100 Largest US Charities list—a lofty perch when you place it alongside the fundraising efforts of more than 1.5 million nonprofit organizations in the country! He also wanted to invite me to join him on a relief mission to El Salvador, which we weren't able to pull off at the time due to security issues, but it is my hope that one of these days I might join Hal in the field to see the power and reach of his good works firsthand.

As for me—well, I'm no longer in the business of being governor, but Hal and I have kept in touch over the years, because there's no looking away from the tremendous impact he and his team are having all over the world.

Let me tell you about it.

Convoy of Hope is a faith-based humanitarian and disaster-relief organization that currently feeds more than 571,000 children worldwide each day—and has served more than 250 million people in total since Hal, together with his brothers and friends, started the organization in 1994. In addition, Convoy of Hope trains and helps tens of thousands of mothers annually to start their own businesses (so they can feed their kids) and provides training to tens of thousands of farmers each year as well. To date, they've distributed more than $2.5 billion in food and supplies in more than 130 countries, including relief efforts in more than 750 disaster areas, or "hot spots," in the wake of man-made disasters, such as wars and insurrections, and natural disasters, such as floods, hurricanes, and tornadoes.

But those numbers, as impressive as they are, don't really tell the full story of this heroic initiative, and in order to do that I believe we need to go back and understand the people-building mandate at the heart of the organization.

(Pay attention to that term *people-building* as you read along—a term that's new to me, but one that's very much at the heart of Convoy of Hope's mission.)

Indeed, what's most compelling about Convoy of Hope is that Hal came to it on the back of a personal tragedy—a personal tragedy that, for me, hits uncomfortably close to home. When Hal was twelve years old, his parents left the house to attend a business meeting, leaving Hal and his two younger brothers and younger sister behind with a babysitter. In an especially chilling and particularly cruel hands-of-fate twist, it's also compelling to note that Hal's life might have taken a different course if the babysitter hadn't been running late.

As it happened, Hal's parents first left the house with Hal and his siblings in tow, because they couldn't afford to miss this meeting. Halfway down the street, his father noticed the babysitter's car in his rearview mirror finally pulling into the family's driveway, so he did a U-turn and doubled back to drop the kids off and let her look after them, as had been planned.

Well, those few moments of stopping and starting made it so that when Hal's parents finally did get going, the many variables that were awaiting them on the road were unalterably changed, and they were soon at exactly the wrong spot at exactly the wrong time. If they'd left the house one minute earlier or one minute later, those variables would have added up in a whole other way.

About an hour and a half after Hal and his siblings had been dropped off back home, two uniformed police officers knocked on the door at Hal's house to deliver the news that his parents had been hit by a drunk driver. Hal's father had been killed, and his mother had been seriously injured and was now fighting for her life in the hospital. Hal says the next moments are a kind of blur, as friends and neighbors started hearing about the accident and showing up in the front yard. They saw the squad cars arrive and they were drawn to the house to see what was going on—and, once they learned what was going on, most of them stayed to see how they might help.

Now, I think we can all recognize this as one of those unbelievably sad stories that tug at our human heartstrings, but I do want to point out that it hits me on a deeply personal level as well. As you might know if you've read any of my previous books or listened to any of my speeches on the campaign trail, I lost my own parents to an eerily similar tragedy. On August 20, 1987, as I was serving my third term in Congress, my parents were pulling out of a Burger King parking lot in my hometown of McKees Rocks, Pennsylvania, when they were hit by a drunk driver. My father died at the scene. My mother died the following day. And just as Hal has been made to live with all of those *What if?* scenarios bouncing around in his head—What if the babysitter had been on time? What if they hadn't doubled back to meet the babysitter when they saw her pull into the driveway after they had left?—I learned to live with my own version of the same. You see, my parents happened to stop at that Burger King because they loved the coffee there. All they wanted was coffee, but what if they had stayed longer and gotten something to eat? What if they had pulled from the parking lot just a moment later?

Of course, I was an adult when my parents were killed, living on my own, already embarked on a political career, while Hal and his brothers and sister were just little kids, so I can only get close to understanding how devastating it must have been for them to receive this kind of news in this kind of way. I can begin to imagine it, though. In my own case, the news sent me reeling, returning me to a life of faith I had momentarily set aside. I started attending a Bible study group in Washington, DC, where I worked, but my parents' death inspired me to start another study group in Columbus, Ohio, where I lived, and soon I was shuttling back and forth between Columbus and Washington, so that I could be home every other Monday, which was when the new group would meet. I wrote about that experience in my book *Every Other Monday*, and shared with readers about my search for meaning in life as I struggled to understand my parents' untimely deaths.

"I was committed to a journey that would help me determine where I stood with God and my eternal destiny," I wrote of this turning-point moment.

Hal's needs were way more pressing—and they were immediately apparent to everyone who turned up at their house on the night of the accident. He and his siblings needed a place to live. Not just for one night, but for the next little while, until his mother hopefully recovered from her injuries and was able to return home and find a way to rebuild life.

As that terrible evening wore on, a police officer stepped to the porch of the Donaldson house and addressed the crowd of thirty or so people on the front lawn. He asked if there were any family or friends in attendance who might be able to take Hal and his siblings home with them. If not, he said, the police officers would have to take the kids down to the station. One young couple volunteered to take them in. Their names were Bill and LouVada Davis, and they were a godsend—and, it would turn out, an inspiration.

"The Davises lived in a small single-wide trailer in a trailer park in town," Hal says. "And they had kids of their own. I'm sure they thought it would be for just a few nights, like a sleepover, but we ended up living with their family for about a year, and they were amazing. They sacrificed their privacy and drained their savings account so the four of us could have a home during this terrible time. They didn't even have enough beds for all of us, so we took turns sleeping on the floor, but to this day I tell people that if it hadn't been for the kindness of people like the Davises, or the people at our church, I probably would have chosen a life of bitterness."

Eventually, mercifully, Hal's mother recovered from her broken bones and internal injuries and was able to return home to get a job.

Check that: She couldn't return home—not to the home she had left, because that house was a rental and the family had to give it up during her long months of recovery, so Hal's mother scrambled to find them a new place to live in California's East Bay area, just outside Oakland.

And check this as well: One job wasn't enough for Hal's mother to make ends meet for her and her four kids, so she ended up taking a second job. Hal's parents didn't have insurance, and the man who hit them didn't have insurance, so it was the beginning of a long struggle for the Donaldson family; they were never made entirely whole after the accident, but they never gave up trying, and they never forgot the many benevolences of their community.

How do you recover from something like that? The best you can do, really, is get by, and that's about where Hal's family landed: They got by.

Hal's father had been a pastor of the Neighborhood Church, a local nondenominational congregation—but, sadly, that church was also lost with his father's passing, when the members decided to merge their congregation with another church nearby. This is the fate of a lot of small local churches across the country when a congregation is left suddenly without a pastoral leader. Still, members of the Neighborhood Church continued to look after the pastor's family in what ways they could—turning up with a new pair of shoes for Hal, for example, when they noticed Hal's shoes had holes in them and the soles had worn through. Or stopping by with groceries, because they knew the cupboards were probably bare. And when the congregants at their newly formed church across town learned of the family's ordeal, they started pitching in, too.

As you might imagine, his parents' accident marked a transformative moment in Hal's young life. Losing his father like that, and nearly losing his mother, and being forced from the family's home—it imprinted on him in a fundamental way that he needed to lift himself from poverty and put back into the world some of the many kindnesses that had been bestowed upon him and his family. As a young man, however, his focus was mostly on the former, and Hal himself would be the first to tell you that his priorities weren't exactly in order when he was just starting out in life, but he would get to the latter in time.

I can certainly relate to that. Like Hal, I'd been raised in a faith-based household. Like Hal, I'd been taught that going to church and praying to God were important touchstones—essential, even—but as a young man I drifted. Once I was out on my own, I stopped going to church, and I no longer prayed all that much, and it took an inciting incident like the death of my parents to remind me of the path I was meant to be walking.

With Hal, that inciting incident set him down on his own purposeful path—one that at first was a little self-focused. Only it wasn't just *one* inciting incident, as we will soon see. It was the way his parents' accident set him up for a chance meeting with one of the world's great missionaries more than ten years later that would set Hal on his present course.

"One of the things that happens when you're raised poor," he explains, "is that you just begin this quest not to be poor anymore. And that certainly was the journey I was on. And I thought, well, the best way I can escape poverty is through education, so I worked my way through college."

Hal had it in his head back then that he would be a journalist. He worked hard to achieve this goal. He studied journalism in school and took writing assignments wherever he could find them. This was back in the era of Woodward and Bernstein, when the life of an investigative reporter was very appealing to a lot of young journalism students. Hal could close his eyes and imagine himself traveling the world, exposing great truths, and helping readers appreciate the scope and breadth of the human condition, and he was well on his way to doing just that when he signed on to ghost-write a book for a group of missionaries in Kolkata, India.

"When I arrived," he says, "they wanted me to interview Mother Teresa for their book, and in the course of my interview with Mother Teresa, she just stops and says, 'Young man, may I ask you, what are you doing to help the poor and the suffering?' You have to realize, I'm in my late twenties, and I'm just starting out, but this is Mother Teresa. I figured I better not lie to her, so I told her the truth. I just said, 'I'm not doing much of anything.' The truth was, at that time in my life, I was really more focused on building my career and building my bank account than I was about building people."

Mother Teresa? Are you kidding me? How many of us get to say that we turned our lives around based on an encounter with such a great woman?

(There's that *people-building* phrase I told you to look out for early on in this chapter.)

Hal went back to his hotel that night and thought long and hard about his conversation with Mother Teresa, and I suppose the weight of that conversation became heavier still as he walked past the homeless individuals lining the streets outside his five-star hotel. The contrast, he says, was startling, eye-opening, game-changing—all of that.

"I just remember feeling ashamed of the life I was leading," he reflects, "and right there in that hotel room, I started praying. I said, 'God, help me to change my priorities.' I talked to him just like I would talk to you, and I simply said that some things have to change, and for the whole rest of that trip, and all during my flight back to the States, I kept thinking of Bill and LouVada Davis and the way they'd taken us in. They weren't strangers, they knew my family, but they were just people in our community who saw that we were in need and wanted to help."

On that flight home, an idea for a book popped into Hal's head—an idea that reminds me of the mission our friend Sister Mary Scullion had taken on in Philadelphia, when she determined to live on the streets to better understand the plight of the homeless in her community. Here Hal decided he would walk the streets after midnight in a half dozen or so different cities—Miami, Atlanta, Chicago, New York, Detroit, Seattle, and Washington, DC. With a hidden tape recorder, he would interview drug addicts, gang members, runaways, and the homeless. He would also ride along with the police on the midnight shift and see what he could see. He couldn't say what it was, exactly, that appealed to him about this project, but the idea just came to him, like a calling, in much the same way that a similar notion had found Sister Mary Scullion in Philadelphia. It was a chance for him to become the same kind of lifeline for others as the Davis family had been for him and his siblings, only first he wanted to understand what holes he might try to fill in the lives of others.

So he set about it.

"In each city," he says, "I would see every imaginable thing there was to see. I saw things and heard things that to this day I've never forgotten. And I came out of that experience knowing what I was called to do."

What he was called to do was change the way he'd been living before that eventful trip to Kolkata and double down on the idea of devoting his full attention to building people—the idea of doing *more* and doing *better* that had found him in that conversation with

Mother Teresa. Sure enough, a short time later he found himself gathering a few friends back home in Northern California and distributing groceries from the back of a pickup truck.

"To this day," he says, "that was probably the most fulfilling thing I've ever done in my life."

After Hal and his group had distributed the last of the groceries, they immediately looked for another location where they might give away another truckload of food. And then another one after that. They knocked on doors at churches and businesses with their hands out, looking for donations. Soon they got to thinking about other things working-poor families or people living on the streets might need, and they started handing out sneakers and other clothing items. From there they began distributing books and school supplies, then offering job training and medical and dental checkups. Wherever there was a need, Hal and his group moved to fill it, all in this informal, ad hoc way.

And the effort just grew and grew. There was no end to the needs of this community, he was realizing, and there were countless communities in the same kind of need. There was no end as well to the creative, resourceful ways he and his group might address those needs.

"We never set out to form an organization to do this type of work," he says now. "But it became necessary because we were growing so rapidly. We went from a single pickup truck to U-Haul trailers to box trucks to semitrucks, and soon we were attracting so many people, thousands of people, that we would have to close down the streets." He explains that his group needed to organize in order to assist with its fundraising efforts and to help address the liability issues that would inevitably surface as they expanded their operations.

What I loved about the early days of this Convoy of Hope mission was how everything came together organically. These impromptu street fairs started popping up all over the area, where all of these essentials would start spilling as if by magic from these trucks, being handed out by the dozens of kind souls the organization was able to recruit to the enterprise. But as we can surely realize, there was nothing impromptu about these gatherings, because someone had to arrange for permits to close down the city streets and to find a way to staff the getting and circulating of all of these goods and services.

This is how it happened in a lot of the extra efforts we're looking at in these pages, just as it is likely the way things might happen for you if you are looking to start your own mission. You'd start small and see where your first tentative steps might take you, before you then started taking bigger and bigger steps as you moved along. With each step, you would develop a clearer idea of where you're headed and what it might take for you to finally get there.

For Hal and company, what they found early on as they grew these pop-up outreach efforts was that there was a willing and able workforce in the volunteer ranks of their local churches.

"There was enormous untapped potential in the church community," he tells. "You didn't have to motivate their people to join you in something worthwhile, because everybody had a Bible, and the Bible already says, 'Love God,' 'Love your neighbor.' But you did have to give them a track to run on. That's where we came in. We were able to show volunteers what needed to be done and to explain how to do it."

After a while the group set its sights on an even bigger outreach event—down the California coast in Watts, a predominately working-class neighborhood in southern Los Angeles—the site of the famous Watts riots of 1965. They put together a caravan of trucks (or convoy) to deliver food and supplies to the area, and they turned the event into a kind of mini carnival, with activities for kids and music and games.

Keep in mind, in the early days nobody on Hal's team was taking a dime in salary, and the individual outreach events and the vehicles hired to service these events were all being supplied by the generous donations of local churches, all of it staffed by a workforce of church volunteers.

Clearly, Convoy of Hope's people-building mission was well underway, but they were just getting started.

All during this time, Hal continued writing books for other organizations—mostly biographies and institutional histories—and his work was becoming well known in and around the church community. He hadn't exactly succeeded in achieving his first childhood dream of building his bank account, but he and his wife, Doree, were keeping ahead of their bills, through Hal's work as a ghostwriter and her work as a teacher. They weren't rich, but they had enough—enough, certainly, to devote more and more of their time to this growing charitable campaign. Then, out of the blue, Hal received an offer to become the editor-in-chief of an international magazine based in Springfield, Missouri, published by the Assemblies of God.

All of a sudden, with this unexpected job offer, Hal saw a chance to take Convoy of Hope to the next level. The position afforded Hal an opportunity to travel the world on the magazine's behalf and a level of freedom and autonomy he had never known in his work as a freelance writer, since he'd always been working on a deadline, at the pleasure of his various clients. It also placed him in the center of the country, where Convoy of Hope's trucks could more easily access distressed urban areas across the United States.

While working for the magazine, with his reporter's notebook in hand, he traveled early on to a remote city in Kenya, where eight hundred thousand people were living in abject poverty with no running water, no electricity, no sewer system. It was there that one of the magazine's photographers turned to Hal and asked whether he'd ever considered taking Convoy of Hope to Africa—a conversation that signaled the start of the organization's international relief efforts.

These days, Hal leads an organization of more than five hundred people, and the Convoy of Hope offices are flooded with requests for assistance from small groups and large municipalities all over the world. It's gotten to where the organization can no longer answer every call for help, so they have developed a series of criteria they follow before deciding to bring an outreach effort to a certain community.

"The challenge isn't trying to find things to do," he says of the position the organization is in now. "It's determining what we do."

Hal and his team have a checklist of questions that must be answered affirmatively before they take on a new project:

1. Is there a local church or other religious institution Convoy of Hope can work through to help staff their relief effort on the ground?
2. Is the organization able to reliably and affordably bring supplies into the area—or grow crops or make purchases locally—to service the identified need?
3. Is there a long-range solution that can be identified to address the short-term problem at hand?

This last is key, Hal says, because when Convoy of Hope moves into an area and starts feeding kids, the organization's aim is not to be feeding *their* children and grandchildren as well. They're out to educate the people they're serving so that they might be more self-sufficient going forward—you know, like the old saying that tells us it's better to teach a man to fish than to offer him a plate of fish to fill his belly.

"It really begins with someone on the ground," he says. "A group on the ground that we can work with, that knows the area, that's fully vetted by our team. We're not going to drop food off the back of a truck and move on. That's just not who we are. It's not what we do. We're looking to bring immediate relief, in many cases, but we're also looking to make a long-term impact. In other words, we're not leaving the job unfinished."

That people-building concept at the core of Hal's mission? It's been the driver behind every initiative at Convoy of Hope, just as it can help to fuel every change you might look to bring about in your own corner of the world. Remember, you can't go it alone, there is strength in numbers, we are stronger together than apart—basically, every cliché that we might cite to illustrate that the power of the group far exceeds the power of the individual should rate a mention here. After all, they're clichés for a reason: In cliché there is truth. And here Hal and his team recognized early on that their greatest resources were the people of faith all over the world, standing ready to give of their hearts, time, and expertise.

I think back to that transformative encounter Hal had as a young man when he was interviewing Mother Teresa in Kolkata and was challenged to consider what he was doing to make the world a better place. All these years later, he's still reflecting on it. "As a Christian," he says, "I believe Jesus wants to help the poor and the suffering more than we do. He's just looking for people who will raise their hands and try to help, so that's what some of us did thirty years ago, when all of this started. We raised our hands and tried. I'm probably the least qualified person to run an organization like this one, but what I've learned over the years is that when you reach out and try, you're not alone. You're actually doing the work of Jesus.

"Another thing I've learned is that you can't try to do these things alone. You can do so much more when you bring others along with you on the journey. And, in our case, those have been the congregations. They've provided the workforce that really fuels what we do, and they number over one hundred thousand each year. They come from more than twenty thousand churches worldwide. That's really the army, the driving force. A lot of times people in government step in under the mistaken belief that they can get some of these things done on that level, but they're fooling them-selves, and they're making a mistake when they don't utilize the volunteer army that's out there just waiting to be tapped."

"At the end of the day," he says, "what's most gratifying is that we've helped to change the lives of millions of people, and we've been able to activate thousands and thousands of congregations. And we've been able to do all of that with God's help. I give him all the credit. We've been able to gather and distribute all these resources and mobilize all these volunteers because of him."

CHAPTER 8

DR. NASSER HAJAR AND DR. NADEEM KHAN

"What More Can We Do?"

What I love about this next story is that it beautifully captures the essence of all the stories in this book and asks us to imagine what would happen if a group of individuals uniquely positioned to make a meaningful difference in their community set out to do so simply because it was at hand and was the right thing to do.

I also love that it came about because a group of professionals bonded by their shared faith and circumstances got together and asked themselves, "What more can we do?"

That's what happened in Toledo, Ohio, when a loosely connected group of Muslim physicians teamed up to provide free medical services to uninsured patients, answering their version of the same question that runs through every one of the initiatives featured in this book.

I spoke with two of the founding members of the Halim Clinic—Dr. Nadeem Khan and Dr. Nasser Hajar—to learn how this caring initiative got started. I was struck by the altruism and generosity of spirit underlining the launch of this clinic. I was also heartened to learn of the many collaborative efforts that led to its opening, including the stops and starts that found these doctors as they tried to honor one of the basic tenets of their shared Muslim faith, which holds that as servants of Allah, creator of the universe, they must be ever ready to alleviate the suffering of those around them.

Indeed, the mission of these caring physicians is embedded in the name of the clinic they helped to start—*Halim*, an Arabic word that carries many meanings and speaks to the wisdom, patience, and gentle forbearance at the heart of this effort and a commitment to care that draws on the character and generosity of the Prophet Muhammad. It's a name that didn't come to these doctors straightaway. At first they were known as the Toledo Muslim Doctors Clinic, which even Dr. Hajar allows wasn't all that creative.

"We're doctors," he jokes. "What do we know about such things?"

The clinic began with an informal WhatsApp group of Toledo-area Muslim doctors who regularly exchanged messages concerning the health-related issues facing their community. When I suggest that it was only a loosely connected group to start, I mean to emphasize that not all of the doctors on the thread knew each other at the outset; everyone knew at least one other someone, but these medical professionals had come to northwest Ohio from all over the world and worked in a variety of disciplines, in different offices, hospitals, and clinics, and worshiped at any one of the seven or eight mosques in the city. And yet this disparate group connected by a shared faith and a commitment to healing found themselves wondering together how they might be of service to those who couldn't afford quality medical care.

That's one of the wonderful things that can happen when people are able to tug on the common thread of faith and find that not only are their values aligned but it is as if they have known each other all along—an aspect of organized religion that doesn't get a whole lot of attention these days. Yes, we affiliate with our local religious institutions to pray and worship in whatever ways feel familiar to us, and to model for our children the principles and practices we have come to embrace, but what we also get from that affiliation is, well, *affiliation*. We become connected in a fundamental and resonant way to a group of people who likely share a lot of our same values, experiences, and hopes and dreams.

Dr. Hajar, a gastroenterologist and the current president of Halim Clinic, remembers that early exchange with great clarity, because it so closely tracked with a conversation he'd been having with his father—a nephrologist in Tripoli.

"My dad was asking me if I remembered why I wanted to go into medicine," Dr. Hajar recalls. "We'd first had the discussion twenty years earlier, but of course I remembered. I wanted to help people who were in need. And now he was asking me again what I was doing regarding that goal, and I couldn't really give him an answer."

The very next day, a retired surgeon named Mohammed Amed posted a similar question on the WhatsApp thread, with a follow-up question asking whether there were any doctors in the group who wanted to join him in starting a free clinic.

There's that question again: "What more can we do?"

Out of that simple call to action, a dozen or so doctors convened to consider the prospect. Among that group, Dr. Hajar was the first to raise his hand and ask to be counted, but he was swiftly joined by cardiologists, emergency room doctors, endocrinologists, and general practitioners, some already retired and others with full-time practices, who all found time to meet to see what they could see. Out of that first meeting there began an orchestrated effort to offer medical care free of charge to uninsured patients in the Toledo area.

Now, as I understand it, there are a great many details that need to be addressed before you can even start to think about offering free medical care. It's not like you're donating food or clothing or pitching in to clean up a run-down school property. There are insurance issues and compliance issues and privacy issues that must be considered—and so this group of caring, committed professionals started in on the considering. As it happened, there were small groups of Muslim doctors operating free clinics in cities such as Chicago, Detroit, and Syracuse, so this Toledo group was able to consider those models as a kind of template for what they were trying to build and call on the doctors behind those efforts for advice.

Understand, these doctors weren't looking to serve the city's poorest community, or the elderly, because those people would have had access to Medicaid or Medicare. "Mostly, we were looking at the middle class," Dr. Hajar explains. "People who had maybe let their insurance lapse or who were between jobs and couldn't afford the COBRA payments. People who were maybe deciding to put off a medical exam for whatever reason."

This gap in coverage for middle-class and self-employed patients is a huge and growing concern in this country. According to statistics compiled by the Peterson Center on Healthcare and KFF, two of our leading health policy organizations, more than one in four adults (28 percent) report delaying medical exams or consulting with physicians on an emerging issue because of health-care costs. On a per-household basis, that number is even more concerning, as just over four in ten adults (43 percent) report that someone in their family had recently postponed or refused to go to a doctor because they didn't think they could afford it.

This group of doctors was out to do something about this alarming trend—at least in their own back yard. In order to serve Toledo's underinsured or uninsured community, they needed a place to set up shop, so while they were getting all their paperwork in order, they arranged for space in a downtown mosque—Masjid Al-Islam—where they were able to bring in donated hospital equipment and medical beds and ensure a certain level of HIPAA-compliant patient privacy as they began offering physical exams, blood pressure testing, and primitive blood testing—pretty much all the basic services patients were accustomed to receiving with their primary care physicians.

Remarkably, this arrangement happened not because the leaders of this project were on the board of Masjid Al-Islam or active in that community. The mosque wasn't opening its doors to one of their own or accommodating a service project that had been started by one of its members. No, the doctors somehow learned that there was this suitable space that wasn't being used, and when they asked if they could set up shop there for the next little while, the directors of the mosque were happy to oblige—another reminder that a good turn can sometimes happen simply because it is the right thing to do, and that you never know what resources lie in wait in and around our faith-based institutions.

Beyond the welcome mat the leadership team at Masjid Al-Islam extended to these doctors when they were getting underway, none of Toledo's mosques have been directly affiliated with Halim Clinic, yet the doctors are quick to acknowledge the support they've received from Toledo's Muslim community in intangible, informal ways—most significantly, perhaps, as a referral source for new patients and volunteers. In this way, the program stands apart from many of the endeavors highlighted in these pages, which have surely benefited from a more direct connection with a religious institution, but it reminds us of the open-ended value that can find you when you align with the tenets of a particular faith, in the company of other caring, committed individuals who walk with you in that faith.

It was a slow go at first, once the doctors were able to get all the paperwork sorted and organize and secure their nonprofit status. The slow roll had mostly to do with getting the word out and letting the community know the clinic was open and available to them— but, eventually, the clinic's appointment calendar started to fill. Still, the doctors worried about how to promote their effort. They started a Facebook page and worked with local business leaders and news organizations to get people talking about preventive health care. However, at one point early on in this effort, they realized that their name, Toledo Muslim Doctors, wasn't exactly serving them.

"What we were hearing was that people thought we were serving only the Muslim community," Dr. Hajar tells. "But, of course, we wanted to serve anybody who walked in to see us. Even today, we have this problem, but we are here to serve the entire community."

In a lot of ways, the launch of Halim Clinic reminds me of the way Sister Joan Dawber of LifeWay Network in New York was able to establish a shelter for victims of human trafficking, serving just half a dozen women at first and knowing that she had the funds to keep the project going for only the next year or so. Here these doctors didn't know how long they could operate out of the Masjid Al-Islam basement or even whether that space would be able to accommodate their effort going forward. They knew only that it was on them to get going and that this was a place to begin—an urgent reminder to anyone looking to start in on a big, ambitious mission to proceed with small, accessible steps.

The initial plan was to open the clinic only on Saturdays—the day of the week when the doctors could most readily volunteer their time, but also the day of the week when they could expect to attract the most patients. Soon they started operating on Wednesdays as well, and when I spoke to Dr. Hajar and Dr. Khan, they shared that they were looking at continuing to expand their hours.

One of the welcome surprises early on was the tremendous response the group received from local medical students who recognized an opportunity to volunteer—and, in giving back, to gain valuable experience as well. Most of these students were enrolled at the University of Toledo College of Medicine and Life Sciences, and they cut across all backgrounds and faiths.

Soon there was an additional welcome surprise: Another doctor, who had read about the clinic and wanted to help, offered rent-free an empty suite of offices in the space she was leasing in a downtown medical building, so the group moved from the mosque basement into this more suitable location. A couple of years later, following a shift in the city's commercial real estate market, the doctor could no longer afford to be so generous and announced she would have to start charging a modest rent, but the clinic stayed on as paying subtenants, because the terms were still favorable and because by this point they had established a toehold in the community and patients knew who they were and where to find them.

(Happily, the clinic was able to find a subtenant of its own and rent a portion of their suite to a local laboratory to help defray costs.)

As part of the clinic's slow roll at the outset, the doctors made the decision to offer only a limited number of medical procedures. To be sure, that decision was largely made for them, due to the realities of our health-care system. For example, they couldn't offer pediatric or prenatal care because those specialties are far more complex than primary care treatment. Also, they were not in a position to offer dental care at first because dentistry requires heavy-duty equipment they didn't have the budget to afford. This last started to change after about a month or so, when Dr. Khan joined the clinic team and led the opening of the clinic's dental practice.

"At first we thought we could see our first dental patient after about a month," recalls Dr. Khan, a local dentist in private practice who was born and raised in Michigan and continues to root for his Wolverines over my Buckeyes. "But it took us about seven months to start it up. It was definitely more of an undertaking than we'd anticipated, because dentistry is expensive."

Donations are the lifeblood of Halim Clinic—most of them coming through an annual fundraising dinner that taps individuals and organizations in the community. (The doctors estimate that 70 percent of their budget comes from the fundraising dinner and in-kind donations, while the rest comes through a series of grants the clinic applies for throughout the year.) The clinic also relies on donations of gently used medical equipment from area doctors who are in the habit of updating their examination rooms to include the very latest in technology and design, even if that means having to replace equipment that's still perfectly serviceable. That's how the clinic was able to secure its dental chairs, X-ray machines, and other tools.

"It humbles you, this kind of work," Dr. Khan observes. "But also, I think, as a Muslim community, we believe we are meant to be good ambassadors. We see people of all different faiths every single day, but sometimes there's a negative stigma toward us. So this is just our way of trying to be goodwill ambassadors and letting the community know that we are everyday people just like them. We're a part of this community. Many of us were born here. We take pride in where we live and in our faith, and when we see a problem in our community, such as the lack of affordable health care, we want to be the ones who are out there doing something about it."

This last is a sentiment echoed by Dr. Hajar, who concurs that a motivating factor in launching the clinic was to signal to Toledo residents that their Muslim neighbors were just as civic minded and bighearted as members of any other ethnic or religious group in town, and that he welcomed the chance it offered to help his fellow Muslims feel more connected to their community—and for the community to feel more connected to *them* in return.

Meanwhile, Dr. Hajar is looking ahead to a day when the clinic will be able to offer colonoscopies and endoscopies and other more complex medical procedures, as the clinic expands its fundraising efforts. The doctors will be helped along in this once they move into their new dedicated facility in downtown Toledo, where there will be room enough for additional dental examination rooms, patient examination rooms, and other expanded offerings.

I first learned of the Halim Clinic through friends and contacts at CareNet, an innovative network of health-care providers in Ohio's Toledo and Lucas Counties, where the clinic's medical chair, Mustafa Jaara, sits on the board. CareNet connects uninsured patients, or those who are not eligible to receive Medicaid or Medicare, with area providers, and supplies bilingual advocates to help patients navigate the health-care system. It's like a safety net for folks who might otherwise fall through the cracks, and the more I learned about the good work they were doing at the clinic, and the ways those good works grew from the tenets of a shared faith, the more I thought we should shine a light on this effort.

What more can we do?

That's the question beneath every call to action, and it struck me as especially inspiring that it came to Dr. Hajar in the voice of his father back home in Lebanon, and at some point during our conversation I remark that his father must be a very wise man to ask him what he was doing to help people in need, in answer to the call he'd first heard as a young medical student.

"Oh, yes," Dr. Hajar allows. "Oh, yes, he is."

But it's not enough for me to put the question back to Dr. Hajar on this. No, we must ask it of each other. We must ask it of ourselves. And, at last, I must ask it of you. Readers, what more can *you* do to move the needle in your community? Who can you ask to join you to bring about a meaningful change? What resources are at hand to help you implement an idea or an initiative that might make this world a better place?

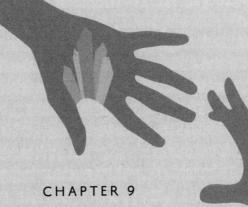

CHAPTER 9

TRACEY BEAL

Fighting Back

Tracey Beal had it tough as a kid growing up in Southern California—in fact, *tough* doesn't even get close to it.

Both her parents struggled with mental illness and alcoholism. Her father gambled and became abusive when he was drunk. Her mother was bipolar, and even though she wasn't physically abusive, Tracey shares that her mother would go into violent rages, throwing things, punching her hand through the wall.

It was no way to grow up—yet it was the only way Tracey knew. The tragedy of her childhood, as it is for so many children in dysfunctional and abusive households, is that Tracey didn't think she had the vocabulary or the agency to speak up about what was happening. As she got older, she was afraid she'd be taken from her home and placed into foster care if she said anything, so she kept silent.

"It's not like we didn't have food on the table or anything," she says now. "My situation was different from what a lot of kids were facing. Kids who didn't know where their next meal was coming from, or if they'd have a place to sleep. That wasn't the issue. The issue for me and my two younger brothers was that we didn't feel safe. I was afraid of my father. I was afraid of my mother. And I didn't know how to ask for help."

The help she did finally find came in the strength of community. By the time her parents divorced, when she was about ten years old, Tracey had found her own way to her local church, where she was able to find a measure of stability and certainty and tap the wellspring of kindness that lay in wait. After the divorce, she didn't see her father again until she was in college, and her relationship with her mother remained fraught, so these church connections were vital—a reminder of the urgency of having a reliable, relatable adult influence in your life when you're a child and a shining example of the purpose that can find you on a faith-based path.

Tracey's involvement with her local church was especially remarkable because her parents weren't exactly active in the community. The family didn't go to church, and it wouldn't be until her mother started watching a Billy Graham crusade on television as she and Tracey's father were divorcing that the idea of observing in an organized way really took hold. Out of that experience, Tracey's mom took her to the Peninsula Baptist Church, where Tracey found wonderful comfort in the company of positive, warm people, who took an interest in her and in her well-being.

It was a place to belong, a place to matter, a place to *breathe*.

All of which tees up the two stories I want to share about this extraordinary woman and the good works she's pursued on the back of her traumatic childhood experience. The first is about the profound impact Tracey Beal has had on the lives of thousands of schoolchildren and their families through an initiative she started called School Connect, which seeks to connect local schools with area churches, businesses, nonprofits, and civic organizations to address some of the most pressing needs in the community. This is the part that has made Tracey a kind of support-systems whisperer, able to connect kids in need with the programs they need. The second is a story about forgiveness—one of the great themes of these profiles, I'm realizing, as I consider them in full. In Tracey's case, her story of forgiveness offers a full-circle lesson in what it means to set aside a lifelong hurt and find a way to heal. Set against the powerful example we saw in the opening chapter of this book, when we met the Reverend Eric Manning of the Emanuel African Methodist Episcopal Church in Charleston, South Carolina, and considered what forgiveness looks like when it is offered by an entire community on the heels of an unthinkable atrocity, Tracey's story tells a far more personal tale and asks us to consider the places we make for forgiveness within families.

I'll offer the big-picture story first, because this was why I reached out to Tracey. The inspiration for the work she would go on to do on behalf of school-age children would have its roots in the many ways she was lifted and supported by the people in her church community when she was a child.

"All of a sudden, I had this group of caring adults taking an interest in me," she tells of the safe haven she found at Peninsula Baptist Church, back when her parents were struggling and her household was in chaos. "Going out of their way for me, even. Literally, out of their way. They'd drive me back and forth to the church, even though they lived in the opposite direction. And as the drama of my parents' divorce played out, I started spending more and more time out of the house, with all these good, caring people, with good values."

By thirteen, Tracey was running many of the children's programs at church, leading vacation Bible school groups, service projects, and mission trips, and the great takeaway for her was that she had something of value to offer—a measure of positive reinforcement she never found at home. The message that kept coming back to her was that she mattered, after being told in no uncertain terms, going back as far as she could remember, that she hardly mattered at all.

"I think, for me, I found community in the faith community," she reflects. "And I also found it in school, where I was able to do well. My response to my childhood and how things were at home was to be very good, and part of that thinking was, you know, if I was good, I would not get clobbered by my parents. If I was good, their focus wouldn't be on me, and I would be okay."

Tracey did so well in school, in fact, that she qualified for scholarships that helped her to attend a private Christian college upon graduation—Westmont College, in Santa Barbara, where she met her future husband, David. Her first thought when she got to Westmont was to pursue a life in the ministry, and with this in mind she studied theology and sociology, but after she and David married, they went to Fuller Seminary in Pasadena, and together they embarked on a journey as church planters, working with a group of churches called the Vineyard, which grew out of a movement that had its roots in Los Angeles in the 1970s and has now become a network of more than twenty-four hundred churches worldwide. As church planters, it fell to Tracey and David to move into a new community and develop foundational relationships with the locals and ultimately start a new church—from scratch. It's an ambitious, endlessly rewarding undertaking, and Tracey and her husband took to it in such a way that it became a kind of calling, ultimately leading them to start a Young Life ministry at their kids' high school.

Do you know about this organization? Young Life is an outreach program for junior high school, high school, and college students, developed to connect uncommitted, disinterested young people to the gospel and provide fellowship and mentorship opportunities that might help them find their way. There are Young Life chapters all over the world, and what I love about Tracey's story is that she was able to attach her own informal experiences at that Baptist church in her hometown, where friends and neighbors and (in some cases) perfect strangers pitched in to offer her a loving lifeline, to a more methodical, more organized program to be of service to young people who may not have been getting the support they needed at home.

The one surely followed from the other and it led Tracey and her husband to found their own Young Life college chapter at Arizona State University, where they started leading service trips to out-of-the-way places such as Peru, and it was while Tracey and her group were working in a public school in Lima, helping to address the many needs of the students there, that she had what she calls her aha moment.

"That was when I realized that schools were a portal to every single need in the community," she reflects. "If you're dealing with foster care issues, or homelessness, or food insecurity, or drug addiction, or unemployment—whatever it is, you can start to address all those needs through the portal of a school. That was the big idea for me, to bring all these resources into the school setting. It just seemed like such a natural way to connect the resources and the needs."

Actually, that one aha moment was a two-parter, because as Tracey thought through the first part, she wondered why she and her group were putting this realization into play only in far-off places such as Peru when those very same needs were going unmet back in Arizona. She returned home and started to apply the model for what would become School Connect to the work she was doing in Phoenix, in partnership with Arizona State University.

"Once I started doing the same type of work here at home," she recalls, "it was apparent that we could build an ecosystem of support around the school. You make sure the principal of the school is in the driver's seat, and that they're the one who gets to say, 'Hey, we want to focus on teacher retention.' Or maybe it's parent engagement, or nutrition, or whatever the issues are in that particular school."

From there, she says, the school community is better able to help students and families tap into the resources all around— resources they might not even be aware of if they had to seek them out on their own.

Basically, Tracey envisioned a hub-and-spoke type of model, where all of these different services and resources and support systems would flow to each child through the school setting, and what's amazing to me is that nobody had really thought to embrace this model and put it to work in communities across the country.

That's how it often goes with big ideas, don't you think? The best ones are built on a simple, elegant solution to a troubling, all-too-common problem, and here Tracey was able to identify a preexisting infrastructure that was already equipped to help students and families unpack a variety of services and programs that might be difficult for them to identify or access on their own.

Now, onto the second compelling part of Tracey's story—the forgiveness part. This is the part I didn't set out to tell, but it became clear to me as we visited that I couldn't tell one part of her story without the other. Recall, I wrote earlier that there was a stretch in there when Tracey was estranged from her father, from the time her parents divorced until she went away to college—a period of about ten years. She had gotten to a place where she didn't think much about him at all, and her mother and brothers were having nothing to do with him, but he reappeared in Tracey's world in a sudden and surprising way. Tracey was touring in a school play after her freshman year in college, performing all over the western United States. At the time, unbeknownst to Tracey, her father was dating a woman who found it a little odd, a little unsettling that he had no relationship with his now nearly adult children. Somehow, her father found out about the play, and the woman he was dating got him thinking it would be a good idea to go to the theater to see it.

"He came up to me after the show," Tracey says, "and at first I didn't even notice him. Then he started getting closer and closer to me, and I'm like, 'He looks familiar.' Then I started thinking, 'That's my nose!' And then I realized it was my father. It really caught me off guard. I didn't know what to say or what to think. We talked for a bit and then he asked if he could come to see me when I was back at school and maybe take me to lunch."

Tracey was nervous about reconnecting with her father, but she went ahead and met him for lunch anyway, jump-starting a mostly tentative, mostly long-distance relationship that would continue for the rest of her father's life. He would call Tracey once a year, on Christmas, and this was how she knew where he was living, what he was up to, how he was doing. He'd gone to AA after the divorce and completed the twelve-step program, and when he got together with Tracey, he apologized for abusing her and her brothers and for wrecking their childhoods—an apology Tracey didn't quite know what to do with at first.

For years, Tracey's relationship with her father didn't stretch beyond these annual Christmas phone calls, but she learned that he moved around a lot and had become a successful real estate salesman, and that he was determined to make repairs. And then, after another ten years or so, he stopped working and started moving around even more. He was constantly on the move, and by this point Tracey was the only one in her family still in touch with him, so she found herself looking forward to these calls, mostly for the throughline they offered from the frightened little girl she had been to the confident, bighearted woman she had become.

One year, her father called with the news that he had cancer. His prognosis was not good. He was staying with a friend in Newport Beach, and Tracey ended up going to California to care for him in the last days of his life.

She surprised herself by going—but then, a part of her knew she was meant to do so.

"I got to see some pretty incredible things," she says of the time she spent with her father as he was dying. "I finally found it in me to forgive him for the things he did to me, for the ways he treated my mother and my brothers, but the most incredible thing was all the visitors who came to see him and say their goodbyes. His friends stopped by and told all these stories of the things he had done for them, the ways they valued his friendship, and I got to see that he wasn't a bad person. He was a terrible father, but he was not a terrible person."

The forgiveness didn't end there.

Before Tracey had gone out to California to care for her father, she mentioned to her mother that he was dying, and her mother said she wanted to talk to him. There were things she'd been burning to say to him since the divorce, and she didn't want him to die without hearing them. Tracey didn't think this was such a good idea and suggested her mother write a letter to her father instead, which Tracey brought with her to her father's bedside. At the appropriate time, she read it to him.

"To the best of her ability, she made peace with him in that letter," Tracey tells. "So that's pretty miraculous right there."

Another miracle: When Tracey finished reading the letter to her father, he turned to her and said, "Maybe we will be a family in death."

And, still, another: When Tracey's mother called to tell her about her own cancer diagnosis, Tracey found it in her to forgive her as well.

"There was this one call," Tracey remembers, "before my mother called to tell me she had lung cancer, and where I answered the phone and out of the blue she said to me, 'I was cruel and abusive to you your whole life. I'm so sorry. Can you ever forgive me?' I was shocked. To be honest, I wasn't ready to forgive her just yet, and I kind of sidestepped the issue and we just moved on and started talking about something else. A couple weeks later, she called to tell me about her own cancer diagnosis, and she started this conversation in the same way, apologizing for the things she did to me and my brothers when we were kids. Again, she said, 'What I did to you, I'm so, so sorry. Do you forgive me?' And again, I didn't think I was ready to let all of that go, but then it's like I could hear the voice of God behind me saying, 'Are you willing?' In that moment, my whole life flashed before my eyes, and I said, 'Yes, I forgive you.' And I meant it."

What I love about Tracey's model of school engagement is that it seems to have emerged organically from her own experience. Think of it: There were so many unseen hands helping to lift her from those difficulties at home, a community of caring she had just chanced upon as a child, and years later she was inspired to re-create that community of caring for others in a more systematic way. It all ties in.

Too, it's inspired by (and fueled by) the Pure Heart Church in Glendale, Arizona, where Tracey has been a pastor for many years. These days, she considers herself a pastor to the city through School Connect, but she continues to pastor individuals in the church. In a lot of ways, she says, School Connect is an extension of the belief she shares with Pure Heart's senior pastor Dan Steffen, which holds that the work of the church should not be confined to what goes on within the four walls of the church. Rather, it should be about supporting local faith and lay leaders to meet the needs of the community—to meet people where they live and help them to fill the holes in their lives that find them there.

With that guiding principle in mind, Tracey and her team have grown School Connect to where it's now operating all across the country—in communities such as San Antonio, Oklahoma City, Colorado Springs, Fort Wayne, and Orange County, California, with an opening in Green Bay, Wisconsin, on the horizon. On the home front, in Arizona's Maricopa County, which serves more than one million schoolchildren, School Connect has the privilege of working with forty-two of the county's fifty-eight school districts.

One of School Connect's most recent initiatives is a programming model they call CAFE, which stands for community and family engagement, a series of roundtable conversations among the school principal and the school's stakeholders, whom Tracey and team call "the village."

Recently, the US Department of Education cited the CAFE model as a "best practice" for faith communities serving local schools—so, clearly, Tracey and her team are onto something here.

Perhaps the best way to understand the impact School Connect has had on the lives of the students it serves is to look at how the program has helped to transform the life of just one student—a boy who'd fled to Arizona with his family from a refugee camp in Africa.

(I won't mention the young student by name here or identify

his country of origin or even the local middle school where Tracey and her team first encountered him, in order to protect his privacy.)

"There were mud-brown walls," Tracey tells, "and weeds growing all around the building. There was a chain-link fence running the whole length of one side of the school, and the grounds were surrounded by run-down homes, many of them drug houses. You could see needles all around the property, and it just broke my heart. I just thought, 'How can this possibly be?'"

At the time, Tracey thought to bring some of her students from her Young Life chapter at Arizona State University to the middle school to interact with the kids, do some maintenance work, and organize some fun, spirit-building activities—and, over time, these college students began to develop pretty strong relationships with some of the middle school kids. One of those middle schoolers was this young African refugee, and Tracey remembers being struck by his backstory.

"He'd fled his country with his mother and brother as refugees," she recalls. "They were running for their lives. His experience was nothing like mine, but we had both come from trauma. We had both found our school as a safe space, a place where we could flourish, where other people were invested in us, and it transformed us."

That young man would go on to become active in Young Life in high school, and at Arizona State University he would go on to become a Young Life leader, and he would go back to serve the kids at his old middle school through School Connect. When Tracey relates his story, you can hear in her voice the pride and joy and lift she experiences when her life's work moves the needle for just one child.

It takes her back, I think, to the many ways the needle was moved for her as a child and reminds her that even though she started out with a set of circumstances that might have doomed her to a lifetime of struggle, she was able to connect with enough of the right people, in enough of the right ways, to find a path to faith—a path to help open up a way forward for others.

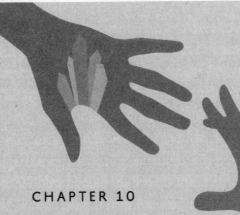

CHAPTER 10

TONY KRIZ

The Power of Partnership

tudents who don't meet proficient reading standards by the end of third grade are four times more likely to drop out of high school without graduating than students who pass those standards."

That's an alarming bulletin from a new book by the Oregon-based theologian and filmmaker Tony Kriz and coauthor Jeff Martin, a film producer and founder of the Children's Literacy Project. I had the privilege of reading an advance copy of their book, *Read: How God's People Can Bring Justice Through Literacy*, as I was doing interviews for this one, and I was struck by the authors' mission to lift our communities by ensuring that all of America's children are reading at grade level by the end of third grade.

Together, Tony and Jeff have also produced a compelling documentary called *Sentenced*, coproduced and narrated by four-time NBA champion Stephen Curry, to help call attention to their literacy commitment, and when I visited with Tony to discuss the film and the book and the mission at the heart of each, I was struck by his team's pledge to offer support and literacy services to those in need by drawing on what they call a "cavalry of caring adults"—a cavalry they hope will number more than one million after the movie is released. I was also struck by the ways their initiative grew on the back of a church-school partnership of the kind we don't often see these days.

Before I tell *that* part of the story, however, I want to emphasize how easy it is to teach a child to read. All it takes, as Tony reminds me, is *patience*—and here I can't help but think back to the many ways my wife, Karen, and I improvised when we were teaching our twin daughters to read. We had no template or YouTube tutorials to follow, no guidepost beyond our own instincts and what we remembered from our own childhoods, yet we figured it out as we went along. That's basically how it happens in the Teach a Kid to Read program, where volunteers are shown a couple of short training videos to get them started, but for the most part they're left to figure it out as they go.

"Grandmothers have been teaching their grandchildren to read since time immemorial," Tony explains. "You read to them and point to the words and help them to sound them out. In a very real way, literacy is so accessible. I'm not saying it's an easy problem to solve, but it's within reach. I mean, if you want to somehow disrupt human trafficking, there are skill sets you need to have, resources you need to have, and most people who want to help in that area would find that intimidating. If you want to volunteer in the prisons, for a lot of people that's really scary and overwhelming. But all it takes to be a reading mentor is to show up for an hour a week, at a school that's probably walking distance or a short drive from where you live or work, and you give them one lunch hour and you walk in with a couple of your friends from your church, and you have this experience."

Stephen Curry's role in the documentary speaks to the strength of this initiative. It came about after Tony and Jeff were invited to present a rough cut of the film at the Justice Film Festival—a leading showcase for films that shine a light on social justice issues and offer a platform for redemptive stories of marginalized communities. After screening the movie to a packed house in New York City, Tony and Jeff and their filmmaker colleagues participated in a panel discussion with several leaders in the field of literacy, and it just so happened that one of Stephen Curry's partners in his media company, Unanimous, was in attendance. She thought immediately of the educational nonprofit that Stephen and his wife, Ayesha, run in Oakland—Eat. Learn. Play.—and she raced from the theater and called the Currys and told them they had to get involved in this film.

She was pretty passionate about it, to hear Tony tell it—and, soon, Stephen Curry was excited as well, despite the fact that the film was already playing the festival circuit. One thing about Stephen Curry, though: It turns out his vision *off* the court is as sharp as his vision *on* the court, because after screening the movie himself with his media colleagues, the basketball star had some notes for the producers. At the time, Tony and Jeff were still seeking a distributor for the documentary, so they were more than happy to go back to their rough cut and reimagine the film and embrace many of the notes suggested by the Curry team.

"Steph and his group were tremendous partners," Tony shares. "They had the idea to add in Steph's narration, and they made some other important contributions, and we were happy to recut the film in collaboration with them. All along, we'd been thinking the film didn't need a narrator, but it turned out that having a voice to tie it all together made such a meaningful difference. At that point, we had only screened it at this one festival. We were still very much a work in progress, so we welcomed the input. And, of course, once you have a film that's produced and narrated by an NBA legend, it raises your platform exponentially, so you do what you have to do to make it work."

Now, the release of the book and the documentary might be the headline heralding this particular effort, but the heart of the story lies in its origins—a partnership that began as a kind of one-and-done cleanup project that paired volunteers from the SouthLake Church in suburban Portland with one of the most underfunded, underperforming public high schools in the city.

What Tony Kriz himself finds most interesting about this alliance is that it brought together parishioners in what Tony calls one of the "least churched" cities in the country to work in support of one of the most neglected schools in one of the worst school districts in the country.

What I find most interesting is that the literacy mission that grew out of this alliance did so in a sidelong way, and quite apart from the hoped-for outcomes Tony and his group had at the outset—an important reminder that sometimes a good idea can lead to an even better idea. In other words, they set out to solve one problem and ended up redirecting their efforts to solve another.

First, let's let Tony explain what he means when he calls Portland one of America's least-churched cities.

"The vast majority of the people in Portland don't identify with any religion," he says. "They've never gone to church and have never identified with Christianity as a formative label. As a result, we have the fewest churches as well, which in turn means that the churches we *do* have sometimes struggle to find a way to participate in society and impact the community—you know, to do what the church is intended to do, which is to love the world."

It was with the goal of loving their community in mind, then, that a group of SouthLake volunteers got together for a cleanup project on the grounds of Roosevelt High School, which just so happens to be the high school Tony's kids attend. And this was no garden-variety cleanup project. It was a full-on, full-tilt makeover—and a much-needed one, at that. For years, the school had been a blight on the neighborhood. The building was falling apart, the grounds were neglected, the students were in and out of trouble with the police, test scores and graduation rates were among the lowest in the country, and teacher-retention rates were also on the decline, so a group from SouthLake, led by pastor Kip Jacob, went to the school and asked if they could help.

Specifically, they asked what they could do to show love to the school community. The pastor had no agenda beyond reaching out with a helping hand and being of service.

The principal answered without hesitation and said that the building and grounds needed a whole lot of TLC.

"My kids should be in a beautiful building," the principal said, "and they're not."

The pastor posted an announcement in the church bulletin—a call for volunteers to help with a one-time cleanup day at Roosevelt High School. More than a thousand people showed up, many of them with their own rakes and shovels and other gardening and hauling equipment.

What happened next was something. In one day, these church volunteers transformed the entire campus. They pulled every weed, scraped every wad of gum off the walls and desk chairs, scrubbed every floor, painted every wall. By sundown, the place was sparkling. By all accounts, the thousand or so volunteers were also transformed by the experience, and they weren't prepared to simply pack up their gear and move on, so on the other end of that effort the school entered into an ongoing relationship with the church. There was a lot of work still to be done, it was generally agreed, and the pastor and his volunteers believed they were up to it. Soon, SouthLake volunteers were signing up to coach the Roosevelt High teams, helping to build and supply a food closet, offering nutritious snacks for the students, and running a clothing closet with used and donated items. Mentoring programs were established, and after-school activities were added to the school calendar—all of it staffed by church volunteers.

Eventually, the school set aside office space for two full-time staff members, paid for by the church, tasked with coordinating all volunteer efforts, setting in motion a church-school partnership model that would soon reach into dozens of Portland area schools.

Tony's role in this remarkable transformation was in helping to get the word out about what was happening at Roosevelt High. As a filmmaker, he led the effort to produce a series of short films about the school's makeover and the unusual alliance that had blossomed from it, as well as a full-length documentary. One of the groups that took note was the Luis Palau Association, an international evangelical organization based just outside Portland in Beaverton,

Oregon, and from there the message of what was happening at SouthLake Church started to spread.

"Long story short, every school in the greater Portland area ended up with a church partner," Tony says. "And every school experienced love in the same way, with no agenda. That was always an important part of it, that the churches weren't coming into these schools looking to proselytize. They weren't looking to do anything the school administrators and parent groups weren't asking for. We were only looking to help. If they asked us to scrape gum, we would scrape gum. Whatever they asked, we were going to do it. It was a beautiful movement."

Word of that beautiful movement soon reached the White House Office of Faith-Based and Neighborhood Partnerships, and leaders in the Department of Education. School-church partnerships started springing up all over the country, many of them inspired by the short films Tony was producing to chronicle what was going on at Roosevelt High School and in and around Portland. Some were now operating under the umbrella of an organization Tony and his group launched called Be Undivided, which was dedicated to promoting these church-school partnerships across the country.

"What we were finding at Be Undivided," Tony shares, "was that once these partnerships were set up, there wasn't much for us to do. They kind of ran themselves. It's almost like we were franchising the idea, and we were of course thrilled that the model was having such an impact, and for a while we thought it would just keep growing and growing. But then, over time, we started to see that church involvement would peter off. After about five years, the gum came back, and the weeds came back, and the new paint started to peel, and the volunteers seemed to want to move on to the next thing."

This, I suppose, was inevitable. After all, when you're inspiring people to reach out and make a difference, it helps if they're able to see the results of their extra efforts. But Tony and his team weren't prepared to watch this initiative run its course. Instead, they looked at ways Be Undivided might make more of a long-term, sustaining impact, and with this in mind they started surveying church and school leaders all over the country to determine the areas of greatest need, where a group of untrained outside volunteers might make the greatest difference. In the end, it became clear that there was one area where their group could make a lasting change in the school districts they were hoping to serve: literacy.

"One in four children grow up unable to read in this country," Tony reports. "One in four! That's a heartbreaking statistic. But what we realized was that our churches were well positioned to help address this issue. Not only that, in some ways we were uniquely qualified to make systemic change, and maybe even change the course of the country, because all you need to be a reading mentor is a heart of compassion, and you need to be able to read."

Some more heartbreaking statistics:

- Sixty-one percent of American children in low-income households are growing up in homes without books.
- Children from low-income households fall behind by as much as two months of reading achievement during the summer months, while children from middle-income homes are able to make slight gains over the same period.
- By age three, children from wealthier families have heard and processed thirty million more words than children from low-income families.
- Eighty-five percent of all teenagers caught in our juvenile court system read at low or very low literacy levels.

Tony points out that since the Be Undivided infrastructure was already in place, the shift required to adopt this new literacy initiative was subtle—more of a change in focus than an overhaul to the group's mission. It did, however, require a name change, so the organization rebranded as Teach a Kid to Read in 2018, and almost all the partner schools have signed on to this souped-up effort, with a dream of putting at least one million volunteers into under-resourced schools, supporting teachers so teachers can go back to teaching again. The Teach a Kid to Read model is still very much a partnership model, calling on local churches to align with local schools and help teachers and students find a way forward, only now the emphasis is on reading.

"Many of these schools are understaffed," Tony tells. "Many of the kids we're hoping to reach come from marginalized settings. They're coming to school hungry, from single-parent homes, where they're not getting a lot of attention. There are disciplinary problems. But when volunteers can come in during the school day and spend one-on-one time with a group of students, and not only help them learn to read but take the time to tell them that they're beautiful and they have a future and they have hope, then suddenly that teacher isn't dealing with thirty kids. Now they're dealing with just twenty-five kids, or whatever the number is, and just like that, the margins start to change."

Meanwhile, Tony's own kids continued to attend Roosevelt High School. On the day we spoke, one of his sons was graduating, and I'm happy to report that at this one school at least the five-year falloff the organization would typically find at other partner schools has yet to occur—more than fifteen years after the one-day makeover that jump-started this effort.

I should mention here that Tony's one of those people who don't just *talk the talk*, as the expression goes. He *walks the walk* as well, just like we saw with Sister Mary Scullion, who doubled down in her resolve to ease the plight of Philadelphia's homeless after living herself among Philadelphia's homeless to better understand the issue. Tony and his wife made the determination early on that their children would attend an inner-city school, be engaged in what he calls "the real world," and have friends and teachers and mentors from different backgrounds. What hasn't changed over the years is Roosevelt High School's location. The school continues to serve a low-income neighborhood in a racially diverse community. But the transformation that took shape on the back of the partnership with SouthLake Church has taken hold in the kind of sustaining ways Tony and his partners envisioned for *all* the school-church partnerships they helped to facilitate across the country.

Perhaps the best illustration of this is the new football field the school's SouthLake partners were able to build.

"When we started out, there was no field at the school," Tony recalls. "There was just a big mud pit. But one of our congregants was a vice president at Nike, and another congregant owned a large construction firm in town, so we partnered with Nike and with the construction firm and raised a bunch of money to build a new football field, a new track, new grandstands, and a new scoreboard. It's now the state-of-the-art high school stadium in Oregon, where we host the state championships. That's the level of commitment we've seen from this particular church."

There's also a new theater, with incredible acoustics, which is now the centerpiece of the school's music program, and the great takeaway for me as I look in on the spirit of renewal that has attached to this one school is the positive metamorphosis that can happen through a meaningful school-church partnership. No, the good people of SouthLake Church cannot change the economic realities of this particular school district. Area families were struggling when the church got involved and they have continued to struggle. But what they *can* change, and what they *have* changed, is the story Roosevelt High students are able to tell themselves when they go to school each day.

"Beauty inspires," Tony says, echoing this all-important point. "It says to these kids that they matter, that society hasn't forgotten about them. The old school sent a very different message. It said that society had tossed them aside, so yes, that's a big deal. It's a big deal that students can show up to school and not be hungry. It's a big deal that they can show up with clothes they're proud to wear. It's a big deal that good teachers are now being drawn to the school, because it's such a good story. And it's a big deal that, with our emphasis on literacy and other academic programs, those teachers are able to fully address the needs of their students.

"When all of that is happening, you're able to think about education more holistically, and the attitude of the entire school community begins to change."

Yes, it does.

CHAPTER 11

FATHER GREGORY BOYLE

The Business of Second Chances

Dolores Mission Church was the poorest Catholic parish in Los Angeles when Father Gregory Boyle was named as its pastor in 1986. The Jesuit parish included two of the largest public housing projects in the country, Pico Gardens and Aliso Village, and the highest concentration of gang activity in a city sadly known for its gang activity.

The parish is located in the coincidentally named Boyle Heights neighborhood of Los Angeles that at the time of the pastor's posting was predominantly Hispanic and Latino.

Father Boyle is well known in the Los Angeles community—and, indeed, across the country—but I'm excited to call attention to his mission here, for the way it so compellingly captures the heart and soul of the good works I've been highlighting in these pages. He was awarded the Presidential Medal of Freedom in May 2024, our nation's highest civilian honor, so it's not like the impact he's been having on his community has been going unnoticed. He's also the author of four books, including the *New York Times* bestseller *Tattoos on the Heart: The Power of Boundless Compassion*, which was hailed by the author Anne Lamott as "an astonishing book . . . about suffering and dignity, death and resurrection, one of my favorite books in years."

Wow—that's high praise, and you might be wondering what there is left for me to write about the pastor, whose parishioners call him Father Greg (or, sometimes, just plain G, when he's in the company of the "homeys" he now so compassionately serves, with a mutual respect that belies their differences). Yet I was so moved and inspired by the transformation he's helped to bring to his community that I feel compelled to share his story, and I'll begin with an overview. In 1988, in an effort to improve the lives of former gang members, Father Greg started Homeboy Industries, which today stands as the largest gang intervention, rehabilitation, and reentry program in the world. That's just the present-day headline, however, and as remarkable as that headline is, the story of how this organization came about is even more remarkable.

It took a couple of years for the program to fully form, with its current name and focus, but the need for such a program was immediately apparent when the pastor signed on. Indeed, he came to the parish with his eyes wide open: Father Greg had spent the previous two summers as an associate pastor at Dolores Mission, so he knew what he was facing when he got the assignment. In fact, he put in for it. He was originally scheduled to run the student service program at Santa Clara University, but after spending a year living and working in Bolivia during the completion of his master of divinity studies at the Weston Jesuit School of Theology in Cambridge, Massachusetts, he expressed a desire to work with the poor and disadvantaged to his provincial supervisor, and he was sent back to Dolores Mission—this time not as a seasonal associate but as the youngest pastor in the history of the diocese.

When he arrived full-time at Dolores Mission, there were eight active gangs in the community—seven Latino and one African American. In those days, many local media outlets refused to mention the names of these gangs in their news accounts, a practice picked up on by Father Greg. He didn't mention any gang by name in his books, and to this day he makes it a special point not to do so publicly. "I don't want to serve the cohesion of the gang," he explains.

He was out to create a different sort of cohesion entirely, and it would spring from the chaos and uncertainty surrounding his church community. His parishioners did not feel safe in their own homes or on their neighborhood streets, and the local youth were at war with each other and transparently at risk. Right away, he knew he needed to engage with the young people in the neighborhood, whether or not their families were active members of the church. "I never saw my parish as parishioners," he tells. "I saw it as geography."

And this particular geography, at this particular time, seemed to Father Greg like a tinderbox ready to explode. "We had kids kicked out of school," he tells. "Junior high–aged kids, middle school kids, and they were making trouble and getting into it in the middle of the day. So I went out to talk to them and I said, 'Hey, if I can find a school that would take you, would you go?' And they all said yes. But then I couldn't find a school that would take them, so that kind of forced my hand, and I knew we'd have to start our own school."

Father Greg is not the kind of guy who sits on an idea, and here he tells how he went directly to the convent across the street from the church and gathered all the nuns for a meeting one evening in their living room. He told them he wanted to start a school for these expelled gang members, which they all seemed to agree was much needed. Then he told them the rest of his plan: "I just came out with it and said, 'Would you guys mind moving out?'" he recalls, putting it out there that not only is this a man who doesn't sit on an idea, but he also doesn't mince words. "And they said, 'Sure, we'll do it,'" he continues. "So pretty quickly we were able to convert the convent into a school building."

When the Dolores Mission School opened, it served approximately sixty students, from all eight area gangs. Father Greg reports that there was a lot of bad blood and simmering tensions among these rival gang members and that in the beginning there were three or four major brawls each day on the school grounds. "I didn't have faculty stay very long," he notes. "I had a principal who lasted exactly one day. When I tried to call him afterward, he'd changed his number and apparently checked into a witness protection program."

Clearly, Father Greg offers this last part with tongue firmly in cheek—the part about the poor guy going into hiding, at least—signaling that he carries the burdens of his parish with great good cheer. There was no denying those burdens, though, and when he was just starting out, one of the clearest indicators of the level of violence in the community was the number of funerals he was called to conduct.

"The first kid I buried was an eighteen-year-old identical twin," he wrote so movingly in his book *Tattoos on the Heart*. "Even the family had a hard time distinguishing these two brothers from each other. At the funeral, Vincente peered into the casket of his brother, Danny. They were both wearing identical clothes. It was as if someone had slapped a mirror down and Vincente was staring at his own reflection. Because this was my first funeral of this kind, the snapshot of a young man peering at his own mirror image has stayed with me all these years, as a metaphor for gang violence in all its self-destruction."

To this day, Father Boyle keeps a grim running head count of the funerals he's presided over—a number that now stands at 261. It's a chilling number he shares in a matter-of-fact way, not because he isn't moved or saddened by it but because he knows that he has no choice but to accept it as a matter of fact in his parish. This is where he works, and this was a fact of life and death in the parish at the time he signed on. Indeed, the years between 1988 and 1998 would come to be known as the "decade of death" among city historians, when there were approximately one thousand Angelenos killed each year in acts of gang-related violence.

You might think, since all of these kids had already been kicked out of the public schools, that Father Greg and his staff would have had a hard time keeping them in the classroom, but despite the daily dustups in the beginning, there was a certain amount of buy-in with this first group of students that the teachers were able to count on as the school year got going. After all, they'd all pledged to go back to school if Father Boyle was able to place them some-where, and now that he'd been good to his word, he reminded them that he was counting on them to honor their word as well.

"Let's say they were all somewhat willing to be there," he says. "They were somewhat willing on some level to make a change in their lives. They were one foot in, one foot out."

The *one foot in* part was key, because in connecting with these strong-willed teenagers and letting them know he cared about them, Father Greg succeeded very quickly in creating a welcoming environment, much to the chagrin of many of the Dolores Mission parishioners, who weren't all thrilled with the idea of opening the church's doors in this way. Soon there were gang members hang-ing around the church outside of school hours. Father Greg helped them turn the garage into a makeshift weight room, and he looked the other way when the Dolores Mission bell tower became like an informal clubhouse, where you could often find a dozen or so teen-agers hanging out, smoking, and passing the time.

"I figured if they're at the church, they're not wreaking havoc in the community," he wrote in his book, but nevertheless the grumbling continued among a certain segment of the community, pushing Father Greg to eventually call a parish meeting to dis-cuss the matter. At that meeting, two influential members of the church rose in support of Father Greg's open-door policy. One of them said, "We help gang members at this parish because it is what Jesus would do."

And, just like that, the matter was settled.

"The parishioners from the projects were mostly women," he says. "That was the profile, single mothers with children. So they were part and parcel of this whole effort, because we'd gone through that whole process of demonizing these gang members, and now we were at this place where they all kind of decided, well, these kids belong to us, whether we brought them into the world or not."

Isn't it amazing, the way the mothers in some of our most

desperate communities, living in the darkest, direst circumstances, can stand with such strength and solidarity in support of their own children?

Very quickly, it became apparent to Father Boyle that what these young (mostly) men needed were jobs, so he jump-started a parish-led program called Jobs for a Future, dispatching hundreds of volunteers to canvas the neighborhood handing out flyers to factory foremen, store owners, and small businesses, trying to create job opportunities. "Basically, we were trying to find felony-friendly employers," he says, "but when that didn't exactly work out, we started creating our own jobs program."

The church launched several in-house projects committed to the idea of hiring former gang members to fill out their workforce and putting them on the church payroll: There was a maintenance crew, a landscaping crew, a neighborhood cleanup and graffiti-removal crew, a crew to help build the church's new childcare center. It turns out there was plenty of work, and as local businesses and nonprofit organizations took note, they began hiring kids out of this program as well.

This Jobs for a Future outreach reminds me of the time as governor that I called for state agencies to stop requiring applicants for state government jobs to reveal on their application forms whether they had been convicted of a nonviolent crime. Our "ban the box" policy didn't mean that applicants wouldn't eventually have to come clean with their potential employers, just that they would no longer have to do so at the outset. Our thinking here was that the move would allow applicants to be judged first on their merits and then be given a chance to explain their particular circumstances—an important reform, we all thought, that came with an important reminder, as we joined fifteen other states taking the position that ex-cons shouldn't be shackled by their pasts, making it easier for them to connect with the kinds of "felony friendly" employers Father Boyle was hoping to find for his charges.

And then, in the spring of 1992, the city was gripped by the riots and civil disturbances that sprang up in response to the arrest and beating of Rodney King. "The whole city just exploded," Father Greg recalls. "Every pocket of poverty was ignited, except for the very poorest pocket, our parish, and when the riots ended, the *Los Angeles Times* wanted to know why that was." The newspaper sent a reporter to visit the parish and talk to Father Greg, who shared what they were doing with their parish-led jobs program, with their second-chance school, and with the sixty or so strategically hired gang members the church had put in place to help still tempers and keep the peace in the projects—a job they took on willingly and meaningfully, because they'd developed a pride of place once they'd found this point of connection in the Dolores Mission community.

Well, that article happened to cross the desk of film producer Ray Stark, at precisely the moment when he was looking to honor his late wife by investing a bunch of money in a local organization working to quell gang violence in the city she loved. You probably know Ray Stark from some of his movies: *West Side Story*, *Funny Girl*, *Annie*, and on and on. What you might not know is that he had been married to Frances Brice, the daughter of Fanny Brice, who was of course the inspiration for *Funny Girl*, and the couple was well known in and around Los Angeles for supporting the arts, local culture, and medicine through the Fran and Ray Stark Foundation.

Ray Stark, who has since passed away, called Father Greg and summoned him to his office and said, "How should I spend my money?"

The appeal caught the pastor a little bit by surprise, but thinking on his feet, he said, "Well, you could buy this abandoned bakery across the street from our school and fix the ovens, and we could put hair nets on rival gang members and start baking bread."

"That was the extent of my business plan," Father Greg tells, once again flashing a winningly wry sense of humor and an unwillingness to take himself too seriously, despite the seriousness of his mission. "Up until this moment, I'd never had any vision of going into this type of business, but I thought of this old Russian guy who had been a fixture in the neighborhood, and he made only one thing. A dark, delicious rye bread he would sell to a lot of the local restaurants. He had come to me a couple weeks earlier and told me he was having trouble finding a buyer and asked if I wanted to buy the bakery. I said, 'With what money? And why?' And then I promptly forgot about it. But then I'm sitting with Ray Stark, and it popped back into my head, and I said, 'We can call it the Homeboy Bakery.' And that was the extent of it."

Ray Stark loved the idea, and the two men shook hands on it, and within a matter of weeks the Homeboy Bakery was an up-and-running concern. A couple of months later, the church reclaimed a tortilla machine in the Grand Central Market and opened up Homeboy Tortillas, and it was at this point that Father Greg decided to shift the focus of the church's Jobs for a Future effort from a job-placement program into more of an entrepreneurial venture. Later on that summer following the riots, with two businesses in the Dolores Mission outreach portfolio, they rebranded their mission and started calling it Homeboy Industries, an enterprise that has grown from a single bakery to more than a dozen social enterprises, including an electronics-recycling program, a catering arm, a silkscreen and embroidery business, an online market, and the Homegirl Café, where "women with records, young ladies from rival gangs, waitresses with attitude, will gladly take your order"—all of them offering employment opportunities to program participants and revenue streams to support the mission.

For a while there, Father Greg even looked to get a plumbing business off the ground—Homeboy Plumbing—but that didn't go too well. "Who knew?" he wrote in his book. "People didn't want gang members in their homes. I just didn't see that coming."

Here again, I'm reminded of the power of connection and the human capital that lies in wait in our own Rolodexes. (Remember

Rolodexes?) Think about the people you already know or the people you might be able to access in a once-removed sort of way and allow yourself to consider the good you might accomplish together. There are all kinds of people in this world—and, at bottom, I believe those people are all kinds of good. They might have assets or insights that they would be eager to put into play on behalf of a *greater* good if only they knew how to deploy them, so if you've got some idea on how to put those assets or insights to work in a game-changing way, go ahead and make the ask. I'm betting that, as often as not, folks will be happy to hear from you on this, if you're able to help them see how their strengths might align with your vision.

If you ask Father Greg what business they're in over at Homeboy, he'll tell you they're in the business of second chances. "Homeboy Industries is not for those who need help," he once wrote, "only for those who want it."

Homeboy's Tattoo Removal Program is emblematic of this philosophy. The idea is to help participants shed the markings of their past lives and smooth out the path ahead—a second chance, or a do-over, to help erase some of the mistakes in their pasts and make a fresh start.

"A lot of those tattoos are alarming," Father Boyle shares. "We would never force anybody to get their tattoos removed, but we make it easy for them to do so. We now run a clinic, Monday through Friday, nine to five, with a whole bunch of doctors who donate their time, and with three laser machines, and when people are ready, they come in and have them removed. It can be an obstacle to employment, especially the neck, face, elbow-down tattoos, or if they have a gang name."

At present, Homeboy's Tattoo Removal Program treats more than three thousand tattoos for more than nine hundred community clients every month. The program is open to participants in the Homeboy Industries program, as well as members of the Los Angeles community, and minors with gang-related or visible tattoos on the hands, neck, or face, at no cost. On its website, the organization likes to boast that no entity on the planet removes more tattoos than Homeboy Industries—a claim I'd like to see someone try to dispute.

Another thing: Homeboy Industries is now a worldwide phenomenon. To be clear, Father Greg was never looking to branch out or take the Homeboy blueprint to other communities, but when word got out of the transformation taking place in and around these projects, the world came calling. The first call came from a group in Wichita, Kansas, who asked the pastor to help them start a Homeboy outfit there. "And so I kind of said, 'Do we really want to do that?'" he recalls. "Did we want to be the McDonald's of gang-intervention programs? And so we said no, but we of course were willing to help them start something in Wichita. We gave what we called technical assistance."

That *technical assistance* has now resulted in more than three hundred programs across the country, loosely modeled on Homeboy Industries. They don't all work with gang members—some of them work in the area of mental health or with disaffected youth, the unhoused, or the substance-abuse population. And none of them use the Homeboy name, but they are all partners in the growing Global Homeboy Network, which includes another fifty or so partner organizations outside the country.

One of the ways you measure the success of a program like Homeboy Industries is the turnaround that happens in the lives of its participants—and one way to do *that*, in this case, is to look at the incidents of recidivism among ex-cons. Typically, you'll see that approximately 70 percent of individuals who've been incarcerated will return to prison following their release. In the Homeboy network, that number has been flipped: Less than 30 percent of the people who come through their doors return to prison.

Another way is to do a head count and look at the number of one-time gang members currently participating in the program.

These days, that number is 575—that's the number of home-boys and homegirls currently on the payroll, working in one of Homeboy's social enterprises. That's huge. What's also huge is that the people Father Greg set out to serve now kind of run the place, and the parishioners who once resisted the presence of all of these gang members on church grounds have now come to be Homeboy's staunchest supporters and most reliable volunteers.

"Everybody holds a piece of this thing," he says.

Still another way is to look at Homeboy's footprint. They started out operating from the Dolores Mission property, but two years after the Rodney King riots they moved into a storefront property in the neighborhood, and six years later they moved their business into an old printing factory. Six years after *that*, they built their current headquarters in downtown Los Angeles, not far from Chinatown.

But Father Greg doesn't look to measure the success or failure of what he's helped to build in a quantifiable way. He simply points to the fact that the program has been around for thirty-seven years, and that it's only growing.

"I don't really believe in success," he says. "I mean, I feel like Mother Teresa on this when she says we're not called to be suc-cessful. We're called to be faithful. So, full speed ahead. I've never healed or transformed any life, but I know that transformation happens here in this place."

CHAPTER 12

CHRISTA CARRERO

Horse Sense

This story starts on horseback. Specifically, on the back of a Tennessee walking mare named Rosie. To hear Christa Carrero tell it, that horse was her safe haven, her inspiration for the work she and her husband, Isidro, do today, running a therapeutic farm for children where vulnerable kids are encouraged to interact with everyday farm animals to help them overcome fear, loss, and trauma.

That farm—HOPE-full Pastures—sits on six acres in Hamilton, Ohio, and matches horses, goats, chickens, and other of God's creatures with kids who are struggling to help them through the difficult times in their lives. (The acronym HOPE is taken from the farm's mission statement, expressing a commitment to restore young lives through expressions of healing, order, peace, and encouragement.) It's truly a magical place—a peaceful rural setting where variously broken children can find a path to healing that seems to have sprung organically from Christa's childhood experiences.

"I would get on Rosie's back," she recalls, thinking back to the dairy farm she grew up on in Okeana, Ohio, "and I would actually ride her bareback, and I would take her out into the pasture and whatever it was that I was facing that day, I could confide in her. I could just let it all out. And that's really where I met God. On the back of my horse. Rosie was the catalyst of healing in my life. Just facing what typical teenagers face. From the time I was in elementary school, and all the way through middle school, I was bullied. And it was something I was just able to release to Rosie. And the beautiful thing about horses is they are the only animals that mirror our emotions. If you're tense, the horse beneath you will be tense. If you're calm, the horse will be calm. And, of course, the opposite is also true. So Rosie would listen and I would vent, and her sense of calm would become mine, and she was just such a great source of refuge for me."

There was a lot going on in Christa's household. She was one of ten siblings, including two children who were fostered from the St. Aloysius Orphanage. Her parents modeled a life of compassion, faith, and service, underlined by a strong work ethic, and Christa took it all in. From an early age she was determined to live a life in kind. In her heart, she knew she wanted to do some type of missionary work, to be a "Rosie" for others, but she also knew that her parents believed she should first go to college or study a trade before setting off on a life of service, so she enrolled in cosmetology school as soon as she graduated from high school.

"It was something I was interested in," she explains, "and something I thought I would take to the mission field, but I ended up getting sidetracked."

That sidetrack led her to a master's commission program in discipleship at Trinity Life Bible College in Greeley, Colorado, where Christa lived with a self-described Tex-Mex family and attended a bilingual church, dusting off her high school Spanish along the way. "I really wanted to immerse myself in the culture," she says, "and to learn as much as I could as I found my way to the path the Lord had for me."

When she completed her course of study at Bible college, she started an internship under the guidance of a woman named Connie Jarvis Sadik, one of Christa's heroes and mentors, who helped to found a wonderful humanitarian organization called Operation Serve, an international ministry that had its roots in a small walk-in closet at a local church in Buffalo, New York, and took on full shape after another of its founders, Reverend Robert Schenck, set off on a much publicized "faith walk" from Buffalo to Mexico and expanded his mission to address the plight of Mexico's young people.

What struck me about Christa when I first learned her story was how adventurous she had been at such a young age. As a father of twin daughters, who are pretty incredible, and a friend to many with adult-age children, who are also pretty incredible, I found her self-reliance remarkable. Think about it: to move to another country, where she hardly spoke the language, to live and work alongside a group of people she hardly knew, to set out to make a meaningful difference in the lives of a whole other group of people who had known only hardship and uncertainty—well, that's pretty remarkable, don't you think?

Christa spent her first summer in Mexico leading the Operation Serve hair clinic there, putting her cosmetology training to work treating head lice and other health-related issues, but also spending time braiding and cutting the hair of the children in her care.

It was, she tells, both an eye-opening and heartbreaking experience.

"These kids, and their families, they were living in and around these garbage dumpsters in Mexico City," she recalls. "It was the first time I'd ever seen real poverty, and we would travel every other week to a different garbage dump within the city, where we would hold our medical, dental, optical, and hair clinics. There was also a team that would do crafts and games and skits with the kids, and it was really such a beautiful thing. Such a hopeful thing. I mean, these wonderful people were making their homes out of garbage, quite literally out of garbage, but they were also making musical instruments, and toys, and finding ways to be content with what they had. This was all they knew, but there was joy in it, somehow, and when I got back to the United States, there was this major culture shock, seeing so much greed, so many materialistic things, so much abundance, up against how these families were living in such desperate poverty."

And so Christa doubled down on her determination to be a light for those in darkness. She was just twenty years old, with a year of cosmetology school, a year of Bible study, and this Operation Serve internship under her belt, and already her path was becoming clear. Actually, I should probably amend that last sentence, because even though Christa's path was apparent, she was a long way from knowing where it might take her—only that her time in Mexico City had deepened her resolve to be the change she wanted to see in that part of the world. Next, she'd go back to Bible college and was eager to grab at an opportunity that surfaced while there to codirect the master's commission in Magdalena, Mexico, since she'd become fairly proficient in Spanish during the months of her internship, and keenly familiar with the Mexican culture. But her parents were not at peace with that plan, Christa reports—a fact of her young life she could only push back on at twenty, but which she has come to understand over the years.

What's also remarkable, and worth noting here, is that even with her evident maturity and personal conviction, Christa honored her parents' concerns about relocating to Mexico on a more permanent basis and looked for a path she might follow on home soil.

It was at this point, Christa tells, that the Lord intervened, in the form of another hero and mentor of Christa's named Linda Kimble, the founder and director of a homeless shelter near Christa's hometown. Here's where Christa's backstory takes a kind of spiritual turn. You see, it just so happened that Christa's mother was inspired by the work Linda was doing locally and the many ways she had helped to mobilize churches all over the world to address the issue of homelessness in their own communities. It also just so happened that Linda had recently adopted two children from an orphanage in Guatemala—one of whom had actually been born in the garbage dumps of Guatemala City.

Christa's mom sparked to that one sad detail about the garbage dumps, connected the dots from Linda Kimble's history to her daughter's time in Mexico City, and arranged for the two to meet, thinking that this one common bond might help her daughter begin to walk a common path.

165

"My mom just dropped me off at Linda's one day and said, 'Bye! See ya later!'" Christa remembers. "We'd never met. I don't think we'd even spoken. I had no idea what to expect. I mean, I had *some* idea what to expect, but I didn't think anything would come out of this meeting other than having a chance to meet this incredible woman and to hear her story and maybe learn from her. It ended up that we had this amazing connection, and she mentioned this need for an administrative director at this orphanage in Guatemala, and the next thing I knew my mother was telling me that I was supposed to be in Guatemala. That it was God's plan for me. Never mind that my parents hadn't been comfortable with the idea of me going off to Magdalena, Mexico. This, to them, was somehow different, and they were one hundred percent supportive of me going down to this strange country I didn't know, where I was only just learning to speak the language."

Almost as soon as she arrived in Guatemala City, Christa's life took another unexpected turn, when she was introduced to a tiny bundle of joy at the orphanage—a one-month-old baby named Adriana. Christa held the child in her arms and her heart opened. She started thinking about her, dreaming about her, praying for her. The people at the orphanage told Christa they'd almost lost little Adriana to dehydration, and in Christa's arms the child seemed to rally, while in her hopes and prayers she grew larger by the day.

Most of the children at the orphanage were special-needs kids, and Christa was alarmed at the level of care. Intellectually, she understood that the orphanage was understaffed and underfunded, but she couldn't shake thinking about these physically disabled and intellectually challenged kids who weren't receiving the kinds of therapies and services they so clearly needed. She also couldn't shake thinking about Adriana, who formed her own special bond with Christa, and within a couple of weeks the little girl was sleeping on Christa's chest each night, in what was essentially a barracks.

"If you've ever been to that part of Guatemala, you'll know the houses are all built a certain way," Christa explains. "They're made of block, but there's typically a gap of about a foot between the walls of the house and the roof, so I would lie there each night, watching these cat-sized rats run across the top of my wall, holding on to this little girl like our lives depended on it. I was terrified, but I knew it was on me to keep her safe, and at the same time, keeping this child close, I felt safe as well."

As Christa talked about her relationship with his little girl, I was reminded of her account of that horse she had in childhood—Rosie, the Tennessee walking mare whose sense of calm had become hers.

Somewhere in the deep connection that was forged on those long, sleepless nights, Christa knew she was meant to adopt this child, so she set about it. Trouble was, she didn't meet any of the requirements that would have made the adoption process go smoothly. "They said you had to be twenty-five years old to be an adoptive parent," Christa reports. "They wanted you to be married for at least three years, and to show a substantial income. Well, I was a single missionary, making next to nothing, so I didn't qualify at all, and if my parents weren't so supportive of the idea and willing to submit their income statement in support of my case, it never would have happened."

But it *did* happen—eventually, mercifully—and Christa and little baby Adriana continued on in the mission field, now a part of each other's "forever family" and open to wherever life's path might take them.

This is where Christa's husband, Isidro, entered the picture. Kind of, sort of. You see, Christa was doing her administrative-assistant thing at the Casa Bernabé orphanage in Guatemala, when she and Adriana traveled back to Ohio for a ten-day visit, and it was while attending her home church, Princeton Pike Church of God, that she met Isidro, who hailed from the Dominican Republic.

"It's funny," she says, "because when Isidro and I first met, I was speaking to him in Spanish, and he was speaking to me in English, and somewhere in there we found a way to communicate."

Somewhere in there, too, they found the point of connection that would define their lives going forward, and almost as soon as they were married and settled in Ohio, they established their own local "mission field," becoming licensed foster parents and dedicating their lives to serving vulnerable children in their community.

Meanwhile, it took about three years for Isidro to legally adopt Adriana, and in that time the family started in on their fostering journey—a journey that was interrupted for a bit when their license to foster lapsed, but they scrambled to regain their certification and continue on in their mission. "Our hearts beat for these fatherless children," Christa says, "and they never stopped beating for them. We never stopped looking for the kids who were in hard places, the kids who were most vulnerable."

As the only bilingual family licensed in their county, Christa and Isidro recognized the need to foster Spanish-speaking teenage girls, and soon they were providing a stable home environment for unwed mothers, siblings desperate to stay together, and other kids in need of guidance and care. Over time, Christa and Isidro started their own family, which grew to include four biological sisters for little Adriana, who soon enough wasn't so very little anymore, and at one point Christa did a head count and realized that she and her husband (and their daughters!) had welcomed thirty-five children into their homes over the years.

"It's really been a full-family effort," she says. "Every time we'd get a call, as the girls got older, we'd have a meeting about it. We would pray about it. We'd ask ourselves if this child was the right fit for us, but the Lord just kept opening these doors for us, and for all these teenage girls."

But this isn't the story I set out to tell about Christa Carrero and her family—really, it's just the underpinning of that story, because at some point on her fostering journey Christa found a kind of throughline connecting the (mostly) teenage girls she and her husband were serving to the child she herself had been, struggling to find her own voice, her own strength on her family's dairy farm. She thought back to the healing, calming presence of her horse, and the healing, calming ways she bonded in those first weeks and months with the little girl she would go on to adopt, and she sought to re-create that same feeling of connectedness for the children in her care—indeed, for the very many children in her community she had yet to meet whom she knew might also benefit therapeutically from supervised interaction with the farm animals and household pets the family had accumulated.

She thought as well about the work of another hero and mentor—a woman named Kim Meeder, who founded the Crystal Peaks Youth Ranch in Bend, Oregon, built on the idea of connecting broken horses with broken kids. That youth ranch became a kind of beacon for Christa as she thought about the ways she might attach what she had come to accept as her calling to what she had also come to accept as her reality. Regrettably, she and her husband didn't have the means (or the space!) to stable a whole bunch of horses, so she remodeled that Oregon mission to accommodate the peaceable kingdom of animals she had on hand.

About that peaceable kingdom, and life on the farm: As her family grew, Christa worked as a stay-at-home mom, while Isidro worked as a plant engineer at Cincinnati Children's Hospital. He also worked on the side as a contractor. Money was tight, and Christa made sure to stretch the family budget as far as possible, which meant preparing all the meals at home and growing what they could on their own. They got their eggs from their own chickens and their milk from their own goat. They milled their own flour. More and more, the life she was living began to mirror the life she had lived as a child.

"I don't think I really realized until I was an adult, until I had my own children, the stability and security that living on a farm can provide," she says. "We had Holstein cows when I was growing up, a total herd of about three hundred, and we milked up to one hundred twenty-five of them on a daily basis. I would help my dad on Saturday mornings as a teenager, and when we were bailing hay, we would work together as a family. We were always out in the fresh air, working and playing in nature, and of course during the week I couldn't help out the way I could on weekends, but I could always feed the baby calves, and I could always make time for my horse Rosie. I started to see the treasure in that, as I got away from it, and at the same time I started to see that Isidro and I had already started to build some of that treasure into our lives. You know, just dabbling in homesteading, with our dairy goats and chickens and turkeys and ducks. We even had some sheep. It just kept growing and growing and taking me back to how things were."

As her daughters grew and became more and more independent, Christa started thinking more and more of how things were for her in childhood, and how things might be all over again, not just for her and her children, but for the many vulnerable children her family had yet to meet. The more she thought about the rich, full life she and Isidro were building on the farm, the more she felt called to open up that rich, full life to others, beyond the community they had been serving as foster parents.

And so HOPE-full Pastures took shape. It was a slow roll at first. Christa tells that she and Isidro had been praying for a suitable piece of farmland for about ten years before coming across their six-acre parcel in Hamilton in 2014, and then for another few years after that they worked on restoring the property and building appropriate shelters for the animals and getting established as a 501(c)(3) non-profit corporation in the state of Ohio. In that time, they reached out to their network of like-minded souls, mostly through their church, calling on them to help raise the funds they knew they'd need to realize their vision and to line up the volunteers they knew they'd need to staff the farm and work with the kids they hoped to serve.

They finally opened their doors in 2020, during the height of the COVID pandemic, and in that first year they served only one little boy and his dad—an encounter Christa credits with reinforcing her idea that the strength of this effort would be in the powerful one-to-one relationships that would form on the back of each animal interaction. I suppose it's worth noting here that the COVID outbreak presented Christa with the final push she needed to see this animal-therapy initiative to fruition. She realized that with playgrounds off limits and the schools shut down, there was really no place for these kids to interact with others outside their home environments—home environments that, frankly, didn't always offer all that much in the way of support. I was especially struck by this because it came about at a time when so many of us were feeling defeated by the shutdown, isolated at home, yet Christa and her husband were able to find light in that dark moment and hope in the face of all that hopelessness. She kept thinking of all the ways she and Isidro might offer a different kind of safe haven to children in need, with therapeutic programming to fill some of the spaces where their other after-school activities might have been.

Since that benchmark first session, the farm has served hundreds of area children and families, and as the organization has grown, Christa and Isidro have reimagined their program to best serve their community—and to match the personalities of the animals on their property. Christa says they're always growing their menagerie, in part to meet the needs of the farm, but also to provide a variety of "partnerships" for the children in their care.

In just a few years, the farm has grown to include a rotation of fifty to sixty-five volunteers, drawn primarily from their own church, but also from other area churches and community organizations—many of whom have been with the program from the outset. And that number doesn't account for the twenty or so volunteers who pitch in to help with barn chores and other work around the farm. It truly does take a village to keep HOPE-full

Pastures going, but at bottom it's those one-on-one relationships that make the difference.

The way it works is each child is paired with a trained volunteer, known on the farm as a "pasture pal," who helps the child bond with a particular animal. Very often, it works out that the child is able to tour the farm and choose the animal she wishes to adopt for the run of the weeklong after-school program, although it sometimes happens that in touring the farm a child might encounter a horse or a goat who chooses her, and the connection is jump-started in this way.

Oh, and Christa's family has grown as well. In January 2020 she traveled back to Guatemala with Adriana, where they met another little girl who touched Christa's heart in much the same way Adriana had touched it more than twenty years earlier, and when I interviewed Christa for this book, she shared the happy news that the little girl's adoption had just been finalized.

Throughout, Christa and Isidro have been driven by their shared faith, and the Word of God is very much at the core of everything they do at HOPE-full Pastures, but the farm is open to all comers, no matter their religious background or affiliation. "Absolutely, we love every person who walks through our doors," Christa says. "No matter what their background is, no matter what they believe. We're here to wrap our arms around them and to be a listening ear, and to let them know that we care. And, of course, our animals don't judge. All they know is to be loving and supportive and compassionate. They're the ones, really, offering this purely nonjudgmental space for these kids, and it's such a wonderful thing to see, the way these kids open up to these animals, just like I did as a girl when I was on the back of my horse."

One of the great innovations Christa has put in place on the farm is that she makes room for the parents and siblings of these vulnerable children to participate with them in the program. "When there's a child at risk, it usually means there's a family at risk," she offers. And so HOPE-full Pastures asks that each child attend with a parent, and sometimes with their siblings, and the staff offers special programming and activities for all of them to do together, in addition to the individualized, one-on-one animal interactions at the heart of Christa's mission.

When I asked Christa to share a special memory or two from the past couple of years, she told me the story of a little boy and the horse he'd chosen as his special animal—a quarter horse painted pony named Jane. The pasture pals at HOPE-full Pastures are in the habit of giving each child a stuffed-animal version of their farm friend at the end of each session, to help them think back on the relationship in a meaningful way, but in this one instance the horse wandered over and made her own goodbyes. Jane nosed her way through the fence and rested her head on the little boy's shoulder, as he snuggled both with this new stuffed animal and the horse who inspired it.

"It was the most beautiful thing," Christa says, thinking back on that memory. "It's moments like that that tell me what we're doing here is worthwhile."

CHAPTER 13

REVEREND PAUL O'BRIEN

One Heart

The shout-out for this one goes to my friend Bob Walter, the founder of Cardinal Health, a global health-care services company headquartered in Ohio. I've known Bob for years and have always admired his passion for giving and building. He and his wife, Peggy, are great philanthropists in and around Columbus, so of course I made it a point to corner Bob when I started in on this book project to see whether he could turn me on to a story I might share in these pages.

Bob's the kind of guy who knows just about everybody, and I was confident he could introduce me to someone who was making a difference in his or her community in a way that had yet to capture too much national attention. As soon as I pitched him the idea for this book, Bob blurted out the name of Father Paul O'Brien of Saint Patrick Parish, a Catholic church in Lawrence, Massachusetts, which was once a thriving American industrial city and is now one of the poorest metropolitan areas in the country.

"He's your guy," Bob said, and then he made the necessary introductions.

Perhaps the best way to tell the story behind the meaningful work Father O'Brien has been helping to do in his community is to first set the scene. The contrast between how things were when the textile industry was booming, when Lawrence was known as "the immigrant city" for the way it provided opportunity and hope to thousands of first-generation immigrant families from all over Europe in the decades leading up to the second World War, to the way things are today is startling. And unsettling. And that's just how it appears from the outside looking in. I can't imagine how it must have been to have lived and worked and grown up in that community and to look on as it was almost completely transformed.

But change is inevitable, right? It's how we respond to change that determines our path going forward, and in Lawrence, Massachusetts, this particular transformation came on the back of a devastating economic downturn. As in so many factory towns, the fates and fortunes of the good people of Lawrence were tied to the good-paying jobs in and around the textile industry. As textile manufacturing moved south, however—and overseas—the population moved with it. The sense of hope that had once been the city's defining characteristic was downsized to a feeling of hopelessness, and as the economy plummeted, it changed the fabric of the community. Opportunity gave way to difficulty. Hope gave way to despair. Over time Lawrence became a predominantly Spanish-speaking city (it's now the second-largest Dominican community outside the Dominican Republic), but the city schools weren't able to adapt to the shift, and without a bilingual system of education in place, students struggled. That's often the first tell as communities start to decline: the underperformance of our public schools and the inability of our institutions to pivot to meet the changing needs of the communities they are meant to serve. This last is key, because if we cannot adequately teach our children, we cannot adequately prepare them for a life of active citizenship, and the cycle of poverty and desperation will only continue.

(In recent years, Lawrence has also become home to a sizable Vietnamese population, transforming the city yet again, this time into a *trilingual* community, and making it even more difficult for the school district to meet the needs of its students.)

Father O'Brien was assigned to Saint Patrick Parish by the archbishop of Boston. It was a posting no one else seemed to want at the time. "You would hope that a Catholic priest would want to be in the tough communities, but that's not always the case," he says with the kind of candor that has earned him a legion of fans in the intervening decades, as well as quite a few critics in the early going. "And it certainly wasn't the case here," he adds.

Typically, a posting like this one is meant to be for a six-year term, so Father O'Brien immediately set to work knowing he didn't have all that much time to figure out the lay of the land. Back in 2001 that landscape was bleak—or, at least, it might have appeared that way at first glance. When the reverend joined St. Patrick's, the church was one of the last Irish Catholic bastions in Lawrence, and there was a simmering tension between the old guard and the new. I suppose this was inevitable given the dramatic cultural shift, but it fell to Father O'Brien to look for ways to ease that tension.

"There was ethnic warfare," he remembers. "The bishop told me to open the parish to the real people of the city, and this approach was not welcomed at all, by plenty of people, for plenty of years. But I was sent here with a mission, to open this place up, to change things up, because obviously the parish wouldn't exist after a certain period of time if it didn't reflect the actual population."

In some ways, even after talking with him for just a short while, Father O'Brien reminds me of the priest at Mother of Sorrows, my boyhood parish in McKees Rocks, where I served as an altar boy. Father Joseph Farina was one of five brothers, all priests, who together served the Roman Catholic Diocese of Pittsburgh from the time of the oldest brother Albert's ordination in 1928 to the retirement of brother Edward in 1994—all told, a span of sixty-six years. Father Joseph was one of those no-nonsense priests who didn't always have the patience for the likes of me. I saw him as the ultimate authority on all matters of the church, the arbiter of what was correct and respectful and expected, but underneath beat a heart of gold and a deep commitment to the parishioners he'd been called to serve.

It was on Father Joseph's watch, in fact, that I first spoke to a large group of people in front of a microphone. One Sunday, at the noon service, the commentator didn't show up, so Father Joseph instructed me to fill in. He didn't ask whether this was something I wanted to do, or something I felt ready to do. He just made a pronouncement and left me no choice, so of course I stepped to the microphone and did a serviceable job of it.

Some years later, when I came home from college one weekend, I was standing in one of the back pews while he was holding the Eucharist during the service and I managed to catch his eye. He motioned for me to come see him after the service, and I met up with him as he was taking off his vestments and he didn't look too happy. I had no idea why he'd summoned me and had naively thought he just wanted to welcome me back home, but that no longer appeared to be the case.

"John," he said in a stern voice, "if you ever come to my church again while I'm holding up the Eucharist and you *don't* get down and kneel, I will come right over and knock you down. You have to honor the Lord. Do I make myself clear?"

I could only nod sheepishly.

Father Joseph came to see me in Columbus many years later, after I had gone into politics, when he was in failing health and in a great deal of pain. During our visit, he let on that he was refusing to take the medications his doctors were prescribing to ease his suffering, saying, "If this is what the Lord has in mind for me, I am willing to suffer."

I'd thought of Father Joseph Farina from time to time since moving away from home, of course, but here I started to see him in a new light. His illness had softened him, and as we spoke, I came to realize what a great impact he'd had on my life as a young boy, continuing on all through my college years. I started to understand that this softness I was now seeing had been a part of his character all along, and that he wore the tough exterior I'd always known only to best meet the tough assignment he faced in our community. That was the way of things in McKees Rocks, just as I was now imagining it was the way of things in Lawrence, Massachusetts, where Father Paul O'Brien had been sent to breathe new life into the St. Patrick's community.

Like Father Joseph, Reverend O'Brien knew not to question what the Lord had in mind for him. He only knew how to meet it head-on, even if what the Lord had in mind for him was a posting to lead this fractured community. As tough assignments go, this one was especially challenging, but the uphill climb was eased somewhat by the fact that St. Patrick's had been holding a Spanish-language Mass for a couple of years before Father O'Brien's arrival and that there was some religious school programming in place for Spanish-speaking children. And yet what the reverend found early on was that the Hispanic members of the church were often made to feel like second-class citizens in these segregated services and programs, which in a very literal sense could only offer lip service in addressing the disconnect in the community. They reported feeling tolerated and accommodated rather than welcomed and valued, so the priority was to out reach these few outreach-type efforts and to recognize that the transformation wouldn't happen overnight.

"I think, for people of faith, they do believe in equality," Father O'Brien shares. "They do believe in diversity. That's what Catholicism is supposed to be all about. I don't believe some of our older, more established members were consciously saying, 'This is our enclave.' I don't believe they meant to be unwelcoming. Some were, but a lot of those people started to leave the community, and the ones who stayed slowly came around to this new reality of what Lawrence had become."

As the makeup of the city changed, the congregation at St. Patrick's was made over along with it, and Father O'Brien worked to understand the shift and to help the members of his community understand it as well. I suppose it was a little like selling beef to a vegetarian—what he had to offer wasn't exactly what the community had in mind. Or maybe a better metaphor would be that it was like offering surfing lessons to a landlocked clientele.

They might not see the need at first to grow their skill set in this way, but when and if they did finally visit the ocean, they'd be better equipped to expand their horizons and experience the world in a whole new way.

"There had been a lot of fear in this community before I arrived," Father O'Brien says. "The people in the church who remembered Lawrence as a flourishing city were concerned. They saw the change as a threat to what was dear to them. To many of them, the Hispanic community represented that change. They'd hear Spanish being spoken and associate it with what was going on in their neighborhoods, with losing their jobs, losing their homes, losing everything. So the thinking was if St. Patrick's goes down that road, then there's no way our future can be good."

That was the resistance Father O'Brien was facing from the (mostly) white Irish Catholic community St. Patrick's had been serving, and to hear him tell it, it didn't come from a place of prejudice or a place of hate. It came from a place of uncertainty, a fear of the unknown, and he knew it was on him to ease his congregants past their insecurities and onto common ground.

He did this in a top-down sort of way, by taking the time to visit with some of the established members of the church and helping them come to terms with the changes all around, but also in a bottom-up sort of way, by rolling out the welcome mat for new members and putting it out there that they belonged.

One of his first initiatives was to close the parish's parochial school and open a citywide public school in the same building. The move was met with some resistance from old-guard parishioners, but enrollment was down at the St. Patrick's school, with a dwindling student population that was still (mostly) white Irish Catholic, and Father O'Brien believed he could better serve the community by opening the doors to a more diverse student body.

It was tough to argue with him, or to go against the facts and the trend lines.

Cut to today, and the school is fairly bursting at the seams, serving a student population that's 88 percent Hispanic. As I write this, Father O'Brien reports that the parish is preparing to break ground on the first completely new school building in the archdiocese in more than half a century.

"If we had not opened to the real community, obviously the school would be closed," he says.

The improvements he's helped to usher in at the parish school would be reason enough for me to include Father O'Brien's story in these pages, but the real reason he rates a mention here is his commitment to ending hunger in his community. This is where the ingenuity I mentioned at the top of this chapter made all the difference. Stay with me and I'll explain. You see, in his first year on the job, Father O'Brien recruited eight volunteers from the church to help him serve a Thanksgiving lunch to the area's homeless community. It wasn't a hard sell to bring people on board to help out with such a thing as this; in fact, there had been a long history of some type of Thanksgiving outreach at St. Patrick's, so in many respects this was simply the first iteration of that tradition on Father O'Brien's watch.

I want to stress here, as the reverend himself makes sure to note, that despite the anxiety of the older members over the changing makeup of the congregation, these were good, caring people, eager to give of themselves for those in need. The luncheon, by all accounts, was a success, but during the food prep and cleanup it occurred to the group that serving this one Thanksgiving meal was just a stopgap measure. A drop in the bucket. A one-time reprieve from an ongoing problem. One of the reasons it occurred to them was because the people they were serving brought it up. They were grateful for the luncheon, and for the kindness and extra efforts of the parishioners, but several of them quite reasonably asked, "What about tomorrow morning? What about next Thursday?"

In the moment, and knowing full well that 75 percent of Lawrence's young people were at risk for hunger, Father O'Brien decided to find a way to keep feeding the community—not just *one more* time but *over* time. His mission statement was right there in Matthew 25:35: "For I was hungry and you gave me something to eat, I was thirsty and you gave me something to drink, I was a stranger and you invited me in."

Already the church was helping to run a local food pantry, where locals in need would line up once each month to load up on groceries. But Father O'Brien wanted to do more. He started researching other ways he and his parishioners might address food insecurity in the community. He talked with educators, hospital administrators, nutritionists—anyone who might have some insight on this issue. He started looking at models that had been tried in other communities with varying degrees of success. And, perhaps most significant, he started rallying the troops, generating a kind of groundswell of support for this big idea to make sure their neighbors weren't going hungry.

For a while, the reverend thought the church could operate a sandwich truck but determined it would be just another drop in the bucket, serving only an occasional meal on an occasional basis to an occasional person in need. He was looking to accomplish something bigger, something sustainable, something that had never really been tried before—a way not only to feed the hungry but to nourish them as well.

"Finally, we decided to do what we should have been doing all along," he says of the flash of inspiration that came from looking to fill this particular need. "We wanted to do the very best for the community, and what we came up with was the idea of a beautiful restaurant. Not a soup kitchen, but an actual restaurant, with really great food, and waiters and waitresses. A place where the people would come in, and there'd be music playing, and a host or a hostess could seat them. A place where they could order off a menu, just like at any other restaurant in town. The only difference would be that there's no check at the end of the meal."

To raise the money to turn this vision into reality, Father O'Brien helped organize a nonprofit T-shirt company called Labels Are for Jars, intended not only to raise funds to build this visionary "meal center," as he and his team started calling the restaurant they were envisioning, but also to raise awareness, signaling that we shouldn't be marginalizing the people in our community by assigning them a label—such as "minority" or "addict" or "troubled teen." The idea was to get us to rethink all the ways we put people into boxes and prejudge them based on the choices they make, or the choices that have been made for them. The T-shirts were stuffed into mason jars, which came with an explanation of the planned St. Patrick's restaurant and a request to fill the jar with money and send it back to the church to help erase the stigma associated with homelessness and hunger.

Talk about ingenuity! The T-shirts caught on—there were ten different designs, and the church ended up raising a couple of million dollars on the back of this inventive campaign, as jars came in from all over the country. What I love about this initiative is that the folks at St. Patrick's weren't *just* relying on the popularity of their T-shirt designs and the proceeds from those sales, they were also counting on their customers to be inspired by the empowering message behind their mission. And when Father O'Brien and the core group of volunteers working on this restaurant concept finished emptying all of those jars and counting all of that money, there was more than enough in hand to fund the build-out of the restaurant, outfit the kitchen, and keep that kitchen stocked for the next long while.

"You have to realize," he remembers, "we had this idea, and we designed this great space, but we had not a dime. Not a penny. Without Labels Are for Jars, I don't think we would have gotten where we needed to be."

Let me tell you about this restaurant. It operates under the name Cor Unum—Latin for "one heart"—and it's quite something.

There's beautiful wood paneling and high ceilings and peach-colored walls. There are fresh flowers on the tables, which are set with fine tableware and linens, and there are even special tables set aside for the many children who show up for meals unaccompanied by adults.

Very often you'll find volunteers taking their meals seated right alongside their guests, so the place has a real community feel to it, where the takeaway is that everyone who walks through the doors of the restaurant, whether they're entering from a place of need or a place of service, is on equal footing. It had always been Father O'Brien's hope that dining at Cor Unum would be more like going out for a family celebration or eating at your own kitchen or dining room table than the institutional dining experience that might find you at a soup kitchen or food shelter.

The volunteers at Cor Unum have been serving two meals a day, every day, for the past eighteen years, and by Father O'Brien's count they currently serve about 250,000 meals each year. Breakfast is served every single day, from 6:00 a.m. until 8:00 a.m., and dinner is served every evening, from 4:30 p.m. until 6:30 p.m. On the restaurant's busiest days, they might serve as many as 800 meals. In the middle of a snowstorm, there might be only fifty guests who show up for dinner. During COVID, when dine-in restaurants were shut down across the country, they distributed to-go meals at the door, and in the wake of the Merrimack Valley gas explosion of 2018, which forced thirty thousand residents of Lawrence and the surrounding communities of Andover and North Andover to evacuate their homes, the restaurant was able to open its doors the next day and offer respite and nourishment to a whole new swath of displaced neighbors.

"We have never failed to serve a meal," Father O'Brien proudly states. "And we have never turned anyone away."

This last is one of the core principles of Cor Unum, but the commitment to serve everyone in the community goes deeper. Nobody's out front guarding the door, making sure you're qualified to eat at the restaurant. No questions are asked. If you show up during mealtimes, you'll be taken to a seat and handed a menu and served joyfully. And plentifully—you can even ask for seconds and thirds!

In all, it takes about ten volunteers for a typical breakfast service, and twenty or so for dinner. Volunteers come from St. Patrick's and other local faith communities, as well as from school groups and civic organizations. The cost of a single meal runs between one and two dollars, and most of the food is locally sourced.

"What we've found," Father O'Brien observes, "is that there is more than enough nutritious, surplus food in this country to feed everybody. If you've got a facility with a kitchen, and if you're set up for it, with the kind of volunteers we've been able to bring together, and the mission we've built, and the resources we've been able to call upon, it's all very doable. In fact, hunger is probably the least expensive social ill to eliminate, if you go about it in the right way."

About the name: Back in 2006, when the restaurant opened, the community was still in the grip of the racial tension and uncertainty that had greeted the reverend when he joined the parish in 2001. "If we had come up with an English name, most of the people we'd be serving wouldn't have necessarily understood it," he explains. "If we had come up with a Spanish name, it would have provoked the Irish. So we settled on Latin, which nobody speaks anyway, and we all loved the meaning of it, so that worked out great."

One heart. It speaks to the collective effort and the shared values at the core of this mission, don't you think?

One heart. It reminds everyone who enters the restaurant that we are all cut from the same cloth, made of the same stuff, deserving of the same bounty.

At the facility's grand opening, Father O'Brien's candor bubbled to the surface yet again, along with his blunt sense of humor, as he proudly showed visitors around and said, "This is like the Harvard Club of Boston, but with more decent people."

Back then, only five years into his tenure, his irreverence wasn't always appreciated by the St. Patrick's community, but parishioners have grown accustomed to his blunt, no-nonsense demeanor. In fact, they've come to rely on it—so much so that Father O'Brien has turned his six-year posting into a lifelong calling. He doesn't see himself going anywhere else anytime soon.

"When my six years were supposed to be up, I kept waiting for a call from the archdiocese," he says, "but the call never came."

Part of the reason for that, he suspects, is that the church had undertaken a number of major-capital projects, including the projected $30 million school building, recognizing that it's a lot to ask of a new priest to figure out how to raise all of that money and manage that kind of budget. But he also suspects that it goes back to human nature and the hard-learned truth that priests are just like the rest of us when it comes to biting off more than they can chew.

"Come on," he says, once again with cutting good cheer. "It's not like there's a young priest out there going to the bishop and saying, 'Hey, I see what Paul's been doing in Lawrence, Massachusetts, and I'd like to give it a go.'"

No, I guess there's not. But there should be.

Just to be clear, St. Patrick's Cor Unum Meal Center isn't the only initiative undertaken on Father O'Brien's watch. It's hardly the most ambitious, in terms of budgeting. Or the most consuming, in terms of how the reverend divides his time in service of this community. But it is perhaps the most emblematic of his impact, reminding his congregants and his Lawrence, Massachusetts, neighbors of the many ways an individual can harness the goodwill of his community and put it to work to fill a pressing need, in a way that honors those in pressing need.

Father O'Brien himself recognizes that impact, although it's not something he spends a whole lot of time thinking about. From time to time, however, he's reminded of it by one of the recipients of his outside-the-box kindness on this issue—and this is where the softness comes in that I eventually noticed in Father Joseph Farina, the priest of my growing up. Not too long ago, in fact, Father O'Brien came out of Cor Unum after enjoying his own dinner there and was stopped by two teenage boys on their way in.

"Hey, it's you," one of the boys said to the reverend.

Father O'Brien smiled, happy to be acknowledged, but unable to place the youngster straightaway.

"I have this disease," he explains. "Everybody looks the same to me, until I get to know them. I don't care if you're white, or Asian, or Dominican. The faces all run together. You know how people are always saying 'I don't see color'? Well, I *only* see color, until I get to know you, and here, with these two boys, I knew from the context that they dined with us frequently, or that they knew me from services, or from school, or maybe from our basketball program. Basically, I knew that they knew me, and of course I wanted them to know that I knew them, even if I didn't *know* them."

The two teenagers—both skinny, both Dominican, both wearing plain white T-shirts—continued on with their familiar greeting.

"Father Paul!" one of them said. "My man!"

"How you doing?" the other said.

Father O'Brien, not wanting to give away his confusion, played along and said, "I'm doing great. How 'bout you? I don't think I've seen you in a while."

One of the boys reported that he'd moved to Florida, where he'd been living for the past three years, and as he shared what was going on with him, Father O'Brien racked his memory to attach the face he was seeing now to the faces he might have seen regularly three years earlier. But before the reverend could connect the dots, the boy who'd moved to Florida turned to his friend and said, "Father Paul here is the closest thing to a father I've had in my life."

"I heard that and thought, 'That's the whole thing right there,'" Father O'Brien reflects. "I mean, for those words to come out of this young man's mouth, that's real. Whatever I did for this kid, whatever time I spent with him, however I was able to serve him, it made a difference. The truth is, most of our boys and girls are being raised in single-parent homes. Most of them don't have fathers, so I'm well aware of the role we can play in the lives of these kids. And I'm also well aware that this kid didn't just turn to his friend and say that I helped him in some way, or that I was good to him in some way. No, he put me in that role, and it's little exchanges like this one that remind me that, whatever moment I am in, whatever I am doing for this community, it can be the most important moment in the life of another. It wasn't about the great meal this kid was about to have in our restaurant. And it wasn't about how I'd maybe helped him on the basketball court or in the classroom or whatever it was. It's that I was there for him, period, and I think a lot of the people who work with us, whether it's in the meal center or in one of our other initiatives, would say a version of the same thing. They would see the same beauty in this one small exchange. The same reward from God."

CHAPTER 14

JILLANA GOBLE AND BEN SAND

Radical Hospitality

As I looked far and wide for stories I might share in these pages, I came across a great many accounts of bighearted souls working in and around our foster care system, setting aside their own needs in order to provide for children in need of a nurturing home environment.

I've already introduced you to Christa Carrero, the young woman who grew up with two adopted siblings among her ten brothers and sisters, and who would go on to foster thirty-five children with her husband, Isidro, on their way to establishing the HOPE-full Pastures therapeutic petting farm in Ohio that now serves hundreds of vulnerable children in the area. But here I want to highlight the good works of two individuals who saw an opportunity to reform the foster care system in a systematic, sympathetic way, looking to take some of the stress and trauma out of the stress and trauma that too often finds our most vulnerable children at this most vulnerable moment in their young lives.

What would happen, they wondered, if our foster care system held a surplus of potential foster families instead of an excess of stranded foster kids?

What if we found a way to reimagine our child welfare offices so that they might honor and celebrate the families they serve?

And what would it mean to the children placed in that same system if they were made to feel embraced instead of warehoused or set aside?

These are just some of the questions Jillana Goble started asking herself after returning to the United States after living for several years in Guatemala, teaching English and providing respite care at a local orphanage. Before she got around to these *big* questions, however, she asked herself a whole bunch of little ones, most of them having to do with the world's forgotten children, and all of them flowing from her own desire to open her home and her heart to children in need.

In answer, she did just that. Jillana and her husband, Luke, moved to New York and fostered their first child—a little boy named Royal. They didn't know a single person who had been involved with foster care, didn't know the first thing about how the system worked and how it didn't, but they felt a calling to make a difference in the lives of vulnerable children, and this was a place to start. At the outset, it felt to Jillana like her calling was within reach—she and her husband would take in a child, and then perhaps another, and perhaps another one after that.

Meanwhile, clear across the country in Oregon, Ben Sand was embarking on his own path, determined to help children in need in his part of the world. As a regional Young Life leader in Portland, that meant mentoring many of the young men in the program—a role he took to joyfully. At the time, Ben was a second-year student at George Fox Evangelical Seminary (now known as Portland Seminary), and he believed he was connecting with the teenagers he was serving—that is, until two of his charges disappeared after being named as suspects in a shooting. All of a sudden Ben didn't know what to believe, or how to be of service, and he studied the parable of the good Samaritan and wondered how he might apply its principles to our modern world, where it often seemed that the deck was stacked against young people born into disadvantage and that no amount of goodwill or good turns could save them.

On the back of that disheartening, disquieting experience, he started asking some questions of his own.

By 2012, Jillana and her husband had moved to Portland, continuing to question their roles as caregivers, all the while redrawing the picture of traditional family—"grafting children from hard places, and their families, into our circle," as she writes on her website. The year after Royal joined their family, they were blessed with a biological daughter, Sophia. The year after that, Royal left their home and fell out of touch—a heartbreak Jillana didn't see coming, and one she continues to mourn—and, like Ben, she was pushed to wonder whether it was indeed possible to make a broken child whole.

Jillana and Ben eventually alighted on the same local faith community in Portland and, with a small circle of friends, got together with leadership at four area churches and decided to "adopt" the local Department of Human Services (DHS) office, with the idea of transforming the culture there. By this point, Jillana and her husband had had a second biological child, their daughter Eleni, and welcomed their second foster son, Micah, into their growing family as well. Too, they found room in their hearts for Micah's biological mother, Jennifer. Soon Micah's younger brother Elias joined them, but he stayed for only a short while before returning to his mother's care, while Micah's adoption was finalized a year or so later.

In her own way, Jillana was beginning to answer some of those big questions as a foster mother, adoptive mother, and biological mother. She was eager to share her insights and experiences with her new cohort, which in the beginning was as much a support group—where they could lift each other up and trade insights and information—as it was an advocacy group. Together, they aimed to bring about change and lift their local child welfare offices from a place of complacency onto a more enlightened, collaborative plane.

I've got to admit, I was thrown at first when I heard Jillana and Ben both use the term *adoption* in recalling how their group started interacting with Oregon's DHS offices, inserting themselves into the conversation in hopes of changing that conversation. I wondered what it meant to "adopt" a government agency, but they filled in the blanks for me soon enough. What Jillana and her husband had discovered at the front end of their fostering journey was that a $10 billion agency like the DHS couldn't possibly meet the needs

JILLANA GOBLE AND BEN SAND

of vulnerable children and struggling families without developing strong ties to the local communities they were serving. Certainly, those needs were different in and around Portland than they were, say, in and around New York City, where Jillana and her husband had set off on their fostering journey, or in my own corner of the world, in Columbus, Ohio. As you might expect in a large government office, there were so many moving parts that were invariably operating at cross-purposes, so many dots that didn't always get connected, so many follow-up issues that couldn't help but fall through the cracks of the system, and no easy way to efficiently navigate the thicket of government bureaucracy. That was Jillana's take, coming to the foster care community as an outsider and recognizing the holes in the system, while Ben came to his version of the same frustration through more of an organizational lens. Together, they came to believe that if this group could get these four local churches to help build a kind of bridge between the state's child welfare offices and the families eager to open their homes to these children, they could transform the foster care system across the state.

Anyway, it was a place to start.

"Our plan right out of the gate was to demonstrate what we called 'radical hospitality' to state employees," Ben explains. "How it really started was going to the child welfare offices with these leaders from our faith communities and saying, 'Hey, we want to apologize that we've been absent from this foster care space.' We took responsibility for the gaps in the system and let them know we would work with them to fill those gaps. We didn't place blame or point fingers. We just said we wanted to do better. We wanted to be a part of the solution."

Listening to Jillana and Ben recount the early days of their effort, I had to admire their approach, because they weren't looking to reinvent the wheel or step outside their lane. And they certainly weren't looking to overhaul the entire system. Mostly, they were out to extend a helping hand, and where they reached with that helping hand were the bottom and middle rungs of the state's child welfare offices, where they expected to find caring, compassionate individuals who were themselves trying to do right by these vulnerable children and their troubled families, despite the fact that they were working within an entrenched, bloated infrastructure that couldn't possibly operate as efficiently or compassionately as the service they were providing surely demanded.

The group's idea of radical hospitality ranged from dusting off an old grill from one of the churches and hauling it to one of the city's child welfare offices to host an impromptu barbecue, just to thank the workers for toiling in what was too often seen as a thankless job and putting it out there that their extra efforts were appreciated, to hosting benefits and fundraisers for families in need or helping to renovate local DHS offices to make them more cheerful, more hospitable. Or maybe the welcoming gesture would be for the benefit of the kids in the system, who were too often treated like case numbers instead of as frightened, isolated children in need of some loving attention.

Basically, they sought to restore a measure of humanity to what had become an inhumane, bureaucratic structure, and they determined to do so with the faith that the way to make a difference was through faith itself—by raising funds and awareness within their home church communities and enlisting volunteers to help them put the *civil* back into *civil service*.

"Just think what was happening to these kids when they were waiting in the office after they'd been removed from the home," Jillana explains. "It's such a difficult, critical time for them. Their parents were dealing with homelessness, or incarceration, or drug or alcohol abuse, or maybe they had an untreated mental illness, and nobody was really looking at what was going on with these poor kids in that time of waiting. There were, like, a million things that needed fixing in the way that office worked, a million things those biological parents needed to be working on, but this was one thing we could address, one place we could make an immediate difference."

With this in mind, Jillana led an effort to produce what she'd taken to calling "welcome boxes"—lovingly decorated, age-appropriate "survival kits" filled with fun personal items and necessities intended to make kids entering the foster care system feel more at home during this particularly uncertain time. Jillana and her team filled the boxes with healthy snacks, art supplies, crafts, toys, a toothbrush, a night light, and a flashlight to help the children feel comfortable on their first night in a strange place, and an assortment of goodies meant to occupy them during the intake process and to let them know they were being looked after.

On each box, Jillana placed a simple affirmation: "You are loved." "You are worth it." "You matter."

At first she got a grant from her church—Imago Dei Community Church—to produce three hundred boxes for her local child welfare office, but the project took on a life of its own, and at last count she and her team have made more than thirty thousand of them, which they've distributed across the state. The boxes became a symbol of the many ways this group sought to transform the state's approach to foster care—and the many ways state welfare officials seemed to welcome these extra efforts.

"Look," Jillana says, "I will be the first one to say there's nothing that genius about a welcome box. But the way these boxes were put together, and the way they were received, told me that God was using this box to shine a light on these kids and signal to the community that we needed to start thinking outside the box on this issue. The boxes put it out there that these kids, who were already hurting, were sometimes being made to wait for countless hours in the child welfare office, and once people became aware of that, they started asking questions. Why were these children being made to wait so long? What was going on in these offices? What can we do to make that process go more smoothly? How can we better attend to the needs of these kids at a time when they're frightened and insecure? These simple boxes became a catalyst for a movement to bring about real change."

The genius behind Jillana's welcome-box initiative was that it sparked a conversation. The kids loved receiving them—and the volunteers working with Jillana and Ben loved putting them together. It was a deeply personal way for people to give back, because volunteers knew the specific box they were working on would wind up in the hands of a specific child and that it would fill a specific set of needs in the life of that one child. That meant it was an easy ask, to get people to throw in on this project. Like many of you, I imagine, I've found over the years that it's easier to enlist volunteers to work with you on a project if you're able to let them know *exactly* how their efforts will make an impact and in *exactly* what ways you'd like them to contribute, and that's what this group was able to do here. One week, a Sunday school class would assemble a couple of hundred of these welcome boxes; the next week, a group of local doctors would assemble a couple of hundred more. It became a full-on community-wide project, as volunteers from the three other founding churches of this movement (River West, City Bible, and Solid Rock) joined the effort as well.

About those renovations to local child welfare offices: Jillana and Ben were struck by the dark, depressing visitation rooms where the children would be taken for monitored reunions with their biological parents. These rooms, to hear Jillana and Ben tell it, should have been like sacred spaces in the fostering community, because this was where parents worked to reestablish connection with their children. It was in this setting that families would begin the hard work of coming back together. These spaces should have been warm, soft, and welcoming, instead of cold, hard, and off-putting. At the time, most of the state's visitation rooms were lit with harsh fluorescent lighting and decorated with cheerless, commercial furniture, which was often in disrepair. It was hardly a suitable environment for families in the system to rebuild these fractured relationships—or, perhaps, to hold on to what they'd once shared—so the group's second major push was to raise church and private funds to embark on an ambitious program to radically remake the public-facing facilities in eight child welfare offices in the community. They canvassed local businesses to donate items to help spruce up these facilities, which led to meaningful contributions from a local paint store, a toy shop, and a framing gallery, and on and on. They even recruited a local sandwich shop to provide lunch for the fifty or so volunteers who turned out to help with these marathon makeovers.

From these informal, grassroots initiatives, an organization called Embrace Oregon was formed, committed to the idea that the state's foster care system was unable to find ideal placements for children or to treat families and prospective foster parents with the care and dignity the process deserved without the support of the local faith and business communities.

The emphasis here was clearly on *community*, and as Embrace Oregon grew, Ben and Jillana and their team started developing foundational relationships with people and organizations throughout Portland—and, soon, across the state. They reached out to local businesses to create partnerships that might align the goals of the organization with the in-kind goods and services these businesses were able to offer. They started working with the state legislature to bring about family-friendly changes to the fostering process and participating in roundtable conversations with DHS leaders, all with a clear goal in mind: to transform the state's child welfare offices into places of dignity and hope and to align each local office with local business and faith leaders to help fill in some of the gaps that DHS protocols didn't quite reach.

One great example of this is the way Embrace Oregon looked to give foster parents a bit of a reprieve from the day-to-day responsibilities of child-rearing, recruiting a cadre of volunteer babysitters to step in and offer them a rare night out on the town—a simple, old-fashioned solution to a core issue facing the fostering community.

In this simple way, with small, loving strokes, Embrace Oregon started to remake the big picture of the state's child welfare program.

Soon the media took note. One local reporter, Steve Duin, wrote an article in the *Oregonian* titled "A Revolution in Portland's Foster Care" that went a little bit viral—or, at least, it went *locally* viral, and the conversation that had started on the back of Jillana's welcome-box program took on even more urgency, while Portland's faith community responded in kind. An effort that had once been centered around just four area churches was now receiving the support of nearly forty.

"The stream turned into a river," Ben was quoted as saying in the article, "and the river turned into a flood."

Trouble was, Embrace Oregon wasn't exactly ready to meet the floodwaters.

"We didn't have a logo," Ben recalls. "We didn't have a website. We didn't have anything. All we were doing was connecting faith communities to their local child welfare offices."

They were also finding ways to meaningfully deploy the big-hearted volunteers from their home churches who were eager to be a part of the solution to what until now had been a mostly unseen, underreported problem.

In 2016, DHS awarded Embrace Oregon a grant to expand its program, which soon prompted the group to change its name to Every Child. The rebrand signaled to DHS offices across the country that they ought to be paying attention to what was happening in the Pacific Northwest. Ben and Jillana hadn't set out to make a difference beyond their own back yard, but the wider fostering community started taking note, and soon leaders and legislators started looking to Oregon for a blueprint they might follow in remaking their own child welfare systems.

"Without really meaning to, we created a paradigm for how church and state can work together on a social issue," Ben considers. "That's why we started hearing from officials in Tennessee, Arkansas, and Indiana. We're hearing from DHS offices all over the country who want to know how to create partnerships like Every Child in their states."

I'm reminded here of the way Ben notes that the organization didn't have a logo or a website when they first started getting attention for their extra efforts, and I have to think one of the reasons their outreach has resonated with people in such a fundamental way is that it came about organically, offering simple, elegant answers to the complex questions facing the fostering community.

Jillana herself notes in her book on discovering the meaning of family, *A Love-Stretched Life*, that one of the reasons the group has succeeded is that its hard work has come from an authentic place. "Looking back over the past decade," she writes, "I recognize that a glossy binder containing a carefully crafted ten-bullet-point plan wouldn't have gotten Every Child to where we are today. It's a mountain-moving, mustard-seed kind of story."

It surely is, and as long as we're here, I might as well share a line from the original mustard-seed story: "Truly I tell you, if you have faith as small as a mustard seed, you can say to this mountain, 'Move from here to there,' and it will move. Nothing will be impossible for you" (Matthew 17:20).

"This has been a national movement," Jillana says. "Ben and his very talented team of top-notch, dynamite leaders are the ones doing our national expansion work, while I'm on the ground in Oregon, doing the empathetic, relationship-development work, and supporting our foster parents through our peer mentorship program."

Perhaps the most compelling part of this Embrace Oregon / Every Child story is that Ben and Jillana are not out there beating the drums encouraging these other municipalities to join their homespun, hard-won movement. No, it's that local leaders across the country are coming to *them*. Their focus has been on their own communities, on the solutions that lie within reach, and that's been the key to their success. They're not out there trying to do too much, but just a little bit more, and then a little bit more after that, and on and on. That's what officials are responding to, I think. They're responding to the ways this group has slowly changed the culture, one case at a time, one local office at a time.

The organization's impact speaks for itself. As of this writing, Every Child is now operating in every county in Oregon. The organization has mobilized more than thirty-one thousand volunteers, introduced more than fifteen hundred certified families into the state's fostering pool, provided nearly one thousand hours of respite care through its Foster Parents' Night Out program, and overseen the makeovers of ninety-eight human services visitation rooms in child welfare offices across the state.

"Ben and I have both lived this personally," Jillana shares. "He has been a foster parent, an adoptive parent. I have been a foster parent and an adoptive parent. And so I think that's a powerful layer to our story, when you take what we're doing out of theory and set it alongside the lived reality of what it looks like to raise your hand and say yes to a vulnerable child."

CHAPTER 15

ERIC LIDJI

Remembrance

One of my first thoughts when I took on this book project was for the victims of the horrific Pittsburgh synagogue shooting on October 27, 2018.

One of my second thoughts was to find a way to write about it that lined up with the themes of this book—perhaps highlighting the good works of someone looking to tap the resources of a faith-based organization to ease the burdens of a community in mourning.

Just to be clear, I'd never really stopped thinking about that shooting and its aftermath—in part because it took place just about ten miles from where I was born and raised, in McKees Rocks, Pennsylvania. If there's anything that connects you to an unthinkable tragedy, it's knowing that it happened so close to home, but here of course the terrible events of that day also resonated because they occurred in a place of worship, while innocent people were gathered in ritual and prayer, and in celebration of their shared faith.

In a lot of ways, I was drawn to this story for many of the same reasons I'd felt compelled to write about the massacre at the AME church in Charleston, South Carolina—the story I chose to open these pages. Recall, for that account, I reached out to the Reverend Eric Manning, the church's current pastor, to reflect on what forgiveness has meant to his community in the wake of the shooting. Recall, too, that Pastor Manning had been working at another church in South Carolina at the time of the shooting and that he didn't receive the Charleston assignment until about a year later, so he was coming onto the scene *after* the terrible events of that day, which had tragically claimed the life of the church's pastor at the time, the Reverend Clementa C. Pinckney.

My thinking with that first chapter was that the good people of that AME church had been put through enough without having to spend a few moments all this time later talking to the likes of me about an anguish they surely wanted to get past—but, also, that there would be something healing, helpful, and heartening to discover in the objective, outside-looking-in perspective of a man such as Pastor Manning, who alighted on a community that was already grieving and desperate for a guiding hand to help them heal.

I was curious to find out how this man had found it in him to heal a broken community—or, at least, to try.

And so I set out to find a similar point of connection here, understanding full well that members of Pittsburgh's Tree of Life synagogue, along with their clergy and lay leaders, had already spent countless hours talking to reporters and historians, as well as to their friends and loved ones and others, sharing their personal accounts of the deadliest anti-Semitic terrorist attack in American history—an attack that resulted in the murder of eleven members of this collective of congregations in the Pittsburgh suburb of Squirrel Hill, at one point one of the largest Jewish communities in the United States. The synagogue was actually home to three distinct congregations—Tree of Life Congregation, New Light Congregation, and Congregation Dor Hadash—and at the time of the shooting members of all three communities had begun their Shabbat morning services, which is what made the story resonate in such a meaningful way with people of faith all over the world.

While those three separate services were underway in the building, a gunman entered and went on a shooting rampage that lasted about twenty minutes, first killing two brothers, Cecil and David Rosenthal, at the main entrance, and then moving throughout the building and killing nine additional congregants. Joyce Fienberg, Richard Gottfried, Rose Mallinger, Jerry Rabinowitz, Daniel Stein, Melvin Wax, Irving Younger, and a married couple, Bernice and Sylvan Simon.

Seven others were injured in the shooting, including five police officers responding to the scene.

Blessedly, there was no shortage of individuals who stepped up in the wake of the shootings to offer guidance and comfort, including the leadership of all three congregations, as well as interfaith leaders from across the city, and as I pored through news accounts of the shooting and its aftermath and spoke with members of Pittsburgh's faith community, I collected many stories of kindness, heroism, and selflessness that attached itself in some way to this story.

There was Wasi Mohamed, at the time the executive director of the Islamic Center of Pittsburgh, who helped to raise hundreds of thousands of dollars to offset the funeral costs for the victims' families and to ensure that the local Jewish community felt love and support from the Muslim community.

There was Rabbi Jamie Gibson, of Pittsburgh's Temple Sinai, who learned of the attack underway less than a mile down the street at Tree of Life while he was holding a baby, welcoming the child into the Jewish community in a traditional baby-naming ceremony, and who in the days ahead would become a fixture of the many interfaith services and initiatives that took place all across the city in the wake of the shooting.

There was Carole Zawatsky, who had signed on as the inaugural CEO of the reimagined Tree of Life center, the dynamic new memorial, museum, and synagogue complex being built on the grounds of the old Tree of Life building, and who in the spring of 2024 presided over the groundbreaking ceremony for the new facility that featured a mezuzah, a traditional marker placed on the doorpost of a Jewish home, made from the shattered glass and scattered debris of the old synagogue building—telling members of the community and honored guests that the mezuzah "will forever be a reminder of our obligation to try to pick up the shards of our broken world."

There was Maggie Feinstein, executive director of the 10.27 Healing Partnership, a collective of mental health professionals offering "support and resources to promote healing and resiliency" to any and all Pittsburgh residents who were affected in any way by the synagogue shooting.

There were the members of neighboring religious communities who invited the displaced members of the Tree of Life Congregation, New Light Congregation, and Congregation Dor Hadash to worship in their buildings and establish temporary congregational homes there, while synagogue members and leadership took the time to mourn and assess plans for their property going forward.

Really, there was no shortage of local heroes who had made it their mission to try to fix what had been broken by this hate-filled gunman—a veritable community of caretakers upholding the time-honored Jewish principle of *tikkun olam*, which can refer to any pursuit intended to repair or improve the world, through acts of social justice, communal healing, or mutual support.

And yet most everyone I reached out to on this seemed to want to remain in the background, even though they'd been at the forefront of some aspect of the Pittsburgh Jewish community's healing journey. I started to wonder what it was about this particular tragedy that left everyone connected to it, and even those only loosely connected to it, reluctant to talk about their role in a public way. I even consulted with members of my own faith circle on this, to get their takes, and I came away thinking that the shooting had had such a profound impact on the city that people were reluctant to give it voice or to become a de facto spokesperson for this sad chapter. I got the sense from the people I spoke to that they were just doing what they were meant to do, or what they felt called to do, and that what they were doing was only meant to honor the victims and their families.

There was something empowering, I started to think, in their reluctance to stand in any kind of spotlight, something ennobling, even though they'd been out in front helping to *repair the world* in their own ways—in many cases, in their own *public-facing* ways.

Ultimately, I came across the work of Eric Lidji, the director of the Rauh Jewish Archives at the Heinz History Center, which for many years had been the storehouse for the cultural and religious touchstones of Jewish life in western Pennsylvania. Eric, like the other leaders I consulted, wasn't looking for any kind of pat on the back for his work in the wake of this dreadful shooting, but the very nature of his work required that he call attention to it. You see, as an archivist, it is Eric's mission to capture every remnant and artifact of historical or cultural moment and find a way to preserve it—basically, to help his community remember what it would be too easy to forget.

"When researchers are studying an event that happened way in the past, they often bemoan what doesn't exist," Eric explains when we sit down to talk about his work, sounding the rallying cry for archivists the world over. "They talk about what they wish had been saved, so here I just thought we should save everything, so that in the future historians and scholars would be able to have everything they needed to tell this story correctly."

Perhaps the best description of an archivist's role in general, and Eric's approach in particular, comes from the journalist Emma Green, who covered the Pittsburgh synagogue shooting for *The Atlantic* and spent some time interviewing Eric for one of her articles. She described him in a profile as "a diarist of small delights, a chronicler of curios, an ardent psalmist of Pittsburgh's quirky charms."

Of course, there is nothing "delightful" about the objects Eric has been tasked to collect for this project. There is, however, something very particular, and thoroughgoing, all of it filtered through the extra efforts of a young man who takes his job seriously and carries it as an honor, understanding that his work and the work of his colleagues will play an essential role in helping to heal *this* broken community.

Recall from our opening chapter that for Pastor Manning in Charleston healing would come on the back of a call to forgive.

With Eric Lidji in Pittsburgh, it would come from a call to remember.

By now Eric has spent more than six years, together with his colleagues and a team of volunteers from the three congregations and other members of Pittsburgh's faith community, helping to curate and catalog thousands of items that have been sent in or left on the site of the massacre: works of art, letters, candles, stones, mosaics, and handsewn items meant to commemorate the fallen in some way. And because we live in a digital age, he is in search of items that can be not only held or touched but scanned and uploaded as well. He is also preserving thousands of newspaper articles, letters to the editor, and social media updates, putting them up on the archive's website so that people can see them.

In the weeks and months following the shooting, items of remembrance were being left outside the synagogue by mourners and well-wishers wanting to express their grief or offer their condolences in some way. After a while, those items started to pile up—and the piles kept getting bigger and bigger. "We had this amazing group of volunteers, maybe a dozen people," Eric reflects, "and they all worked tirelessly carrying these items in from outside, drying them off from the rain, setting them aside. It was cold, it was damp, everyone was heartbroken.

"It's very easy to focus on the people who are professionally doing the work, but they're able to do that only because there's a larger community of people who are supporting it and validating it and encouraging it. It's not just the objects themselves that can be healing, but the act of coming together to collect these objects can be healing for people. That's one of the first things I noticed, when we started out, the way the archive itself has been a tool for helping to build and sustain community."

Let me tell you about those stones that began to accumulate on the synagogue grounds. In the Jewish tradition, there is a custom of leaving a visitation stone on the headstones of a Jewish grave.

It's considered a sacred act of remembrance and a show of respect for the deceased, and here it inevitably happened that as mourners showed up at the Tree of Life building following the shootings, many of them placed a stone or rock on or alongside one of the eleven Jewish stars that had been placed on temple grounds to memorialize the victims. You have to pause for a moment to picture this, because it wasn't just a handful of people who honored the victims in this way. No, thousands of people did this. Many collected beautiful, smoothed-over stones to contribute to the memorial, and some took the trouble to decorate their stones with artwork or personal messages before heading over to pay their respects, but many more simply arrived at the temple without realizing this practice was being observed and wound up pinching a small pebble or two from the gravel driveways of synagogue neighbors.

"People were just grabbing stones on their way over and leaving those on the site," Eric recalls.

Each and every one of those stones eventually made it into the archive.

That's pretty remarkable, don't you think? And that's just one example of the scope and sweep of the open-ended memorial Eric Lidji and his team have been creating, almost from the moment the news of the attack started to spread.

One of the things that struck me when I visited the archive with Eric and had a chance to see and touch and consider many of the items he and his team have collected was the volume of donations sent in by Christians from all over the world. This, too, was pretty remarkable, and I found myself thinking long and hard about what this might mean—you know, to understand the ways this tragedy affected the larger faith community. What I came away with was the idea that this attack had resonated for people of *all* faiths as an assault on religious freedom. It wasn't *just* an anti-Semitic attack. When this sanctuary was destroyed and all these people were killed, Christians and Muslims and others could relate to it because it was a violation of the sanctuary ideal, an attack on the sanctity of faith and the holiness of a place of worship. The outpouring came from the fact that people saw this as a threat to all persons of faith, and in their response they seemed to be saying that nothing can diminish the peace and security and strength we find in our faith—whatever that faith happens to be or however we choose to practice it.

"It didn't occur to me that this would become a professional issue for me until the afternoon of the shooting," Eric recalls as we turn our conversation to how this *heartbreaking* breaking-news story went from a headline to a consuming professional passion. "Until I heard this statement on the news from a spokesperson for the ADL"—the Anti-Defamation League, an organization devoted to protecting Jews from acts of anti-Semitism and highlighting those acts—"calling this the deadliest anti-Semitic incident in American history. Up until that time, I was just thinking of it as this terrible thing that happened in my community, and I was just trying to process it on that level, but all of a sudden I started to see how important it was for me to start documenting the incident at work."

And so, on that very afternoon, while the Tree of Life synagogue property was still considered a crime scene, and while members of those three congregations were reeling along with members of the wider Pittsburgh Jewish community and the American Jewish community, and Jews all over the world, the October 27 Archive was born—an offshoot of the work Eric had already been doing that would soon become an all-consuming pursuit.

When I ask Eric to help me understand the value in assembling such a treasure trove of keepsakes and artifacts, including so many duplicate items or objects of no apparent significance, he offers up a short course on the Jewish understanding of memory. "I think a lot of time we talk about memory as something that's passive," he tells, "but, really, it's a proactive choice. When people say it's something they'll never forget, what they're really saying is that something is so impactful your mind won't let you forget it. In Judaism, that choice might get made through the observance of a particular ritual, where you make a decision about what you're going to remember and how you're going to remember it."

He continues: "In this case, following a crime that is so large in scope that the only way to counterbalance it is in the magnitude of the response to it, you recognize that no single object can stand up to the size of what was done. You really need to understand the impact of it on a large-scale level. How far the pain reached, how deep it reached. And the only way you can do that is by honoring every single individual expression of grief or solidarity or hope, or whatever it is. And it's only then when you can see it all together that it has some counterbalancing weight to it. That's the ethos of what we're trying to do."

How Eric came to this type of work is kind of interesting. He'd grown up in Pittsburgh, and after graduating from the University of Pittsburgh, he started working as a journalist. For a number of years he'd had some success and stability as a freelancer, but after a while he grew tired of the grind of reporting and began looking for a more fulfilling way to spend his days. He started volunteering at the Rauh Jewish Archives, as he says, "just to have something on my calendar each week that I could look forward to."

As it happened, a researcher quit and Eric was asked to take on more responsibilities, and then the archive received a grant that opened up another opportunity. "I just kept saying yes and yes to things," he tells, "and after a while I'd developed a real feel for the way the archive operates, and then when the director left, I applied for the job."

He got the job on November 1, 2017—almost a year to the day before the Tree of Life shooting.

It's a job he wouldn't trade for anything—especially now.

"You know, when I was a journalist, the thing I always liked least about the job was the storytelling part," he says. "I always felt, as a journalist, you're never really getting the full story. You're just doing your best to get as much of the story as the present moment allows. But you know that in the future people will talk about things that they're not willing to talk about now, or maybe documents will surface later on, or whatever it is. That's why history is often more fleshed out than day-to-day journalism. And in what we're doing at the archive, we're really just reporting. We're not doing the writing. And I think there's something really profound about that, about just taking in the facts and putting them over here and preparing them for somebody else to do that storytelling at a later point. When you're just dealing with the basic units of history, primary-source materials, you're allowing people to have a multiplicity of understandings and interpretations of something. It's an incredibly democratic process in a lot of ways."

As part of his job, Eric makes about forty to fifty presentations each year to school groups, local organizations, families, and church and synagogue communities, offering insights into the evolving memorial he and his team have been creating. One of the questions he's most often asked is to identify the most compelling item that's crossed his path since he started this work. It's a question he tries to deflect, because the most compelling aspect for him is the sheer volume of artifacts that have come his way. But there are two pieces he sometimes brings with him to these presentations to signify what he has come to believe is the essence of his emerging collection. The first is a quilted challah cover that was mailed to the Tree of Life offices months after the shooting. Challah is a special braided bread that's typically served on occasions such as the Sabbath or major Jewish holidays, and in many Jewish homes it's often covered by a cloth or quilt, sometimes family heirlooms, until the blessing over the bread is offered.

The quilted cover had been sent in by a non-Jewish woman who came into her living room one day to find her husband watching the news on television while a story was being aired about the Pittsburgh synagogue shooting. She noticed that her husband was crying, and she was moved by his tears—so moved, in fact, that she immediately started thinking there must be something she could do to honor the victims and help to uphold their traditions, while at the same time honoring her husband and supporting him in his grief, and she decided to create this beautiful object—a lovingly crafted piece of Judaica that eventually found its way into the archive.

"I always find it fascinating how when people are willing to be vulnerable, it can often lead to this chain of vulnerability," Eric explains of his connection to this item. "Here this husband, when this moment in the news happened, he felt it personally. And then, because he felt it personally, his wife, who loves him, she felt it personally, and then she felt compelled to do this one lovely thing, to maybe connect them to this community in some way. And so to me this challah cover is a good example of what these artifacts are capable of communicating and the collective story they're able to tell. It helps us to understand the ways we are able to open our hearts."

The second item Eric usually brings with him is an old Torah cover that was sent in by congregants at a synagogue in Istanbul that had twice been victimized in an anti-Semitic attack, resulting in a number of casualties.

"It was their way of telling this congregation on the other side of the world that there's a religious life after these horrific events," Eric explains. "They didn't send an object that had been created after those attacks, but one that had survived those attacks, and one that was central to that synagogue community. This is the garment that covers the Torah, the central text of Jewish life. And in this cover I see something that's central to our sense of intercommunal identity. Here we have this group of Jews reaching out to this other group of Jews, telling them it's going to be okay and that the religious core of their lives will not be upended by this one event."

When I stopped by to tour the collection and learn more about this essential work, Eric had just recently hosted a group of high school students at the archive—the first school group to visit the collection on-site since he began this indispensable work—and what he found was a template for the healing conversations that can happen when the collection is considered in full.

"These objects provide a gentle way for us to enter into these important conversations," he reflects. "They're not violent. The images are not hard to look at. The emotions they hold can be really intense, but that's just because it's hard to sit with the grief of other people. But when these students sat with these objects and read the letters that came with them, they were able to understand what might motivate someone to send a gesture of consolation to a total stranger in another city, and to maybe think what it would take for them to do that for somebody else."

To hear Eric tell it, the work of the archive is never ending, because each day brings something new to consider. And now, with construction of the Tree of Life memorial and synagogue complex underway, and with plans for the Tree of Life Congregation to once again make its home within its walls (the New Light Congregation and Congregation Dor Hadash have decided not to return to the building once it reopens), he has been pushed to consider what items might be suitable for the on-site museum being planned on the property.

"An archive like ours operates only because people want to contribute to it," he says. "And in this case, we operate only because the community is ratifying our existence every day. They wanted these items to be saved, and they wanted them to be shared. The collection reflects whatever is happening in the community. It's religious and spiritual, but it's also economic and philanthropic. It's artistic, it's athletic, it's cultural, it's all the different streams of Judaism, all the ways people express their Jewish identity."

And, as Eric Lidji is learning, all the ways they choose to remember.

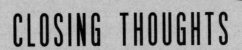

CLOSING THOUGHTS

The "Exclamation Point" That Punctuates Our Faith!

There are a lot of reasons to think our glasses might be half-empty. Or half-full. To measure what we *don't* have instead of what we *do* have. What we *can't* do instead of what we *can* do.

Our world is complicated—I get that. And difficult at times—I get *that*, too. Life can be like a roller-coaster ride, so we must buckle up and lean in to its twists and turns and accept its ups and downs. We must learn to navigate the experiences that come to us in pain and in triumph, understanding that with hope and perspective everything will work out—maybe not here on earth but in the hereafter.

At bottom, this is a book about faith—but if you've read this far, I suspect you already know this. Really, it's about a shining faith that helps people see through obstacles and doubts and to the road ahead, and to know that their ideas and dreams can be realized. It's a book that highlights the good works of people who believe in a higher power that in a mystical way directs and supports them.

What is faith, after all? The best definition I've come across is that it's the ability to believe in something not yet seen. The people you've met in these pages are all people of faith, and all of them were blessed at some point with the firm belief that they could accomplish something they couldn't see—in some cases, something they couldn't even imagine.

Now, too many people have been stepping away of late from organized religion, which in its vital mission can accentuate and reinforce faith, and this is troubling to me. Perhaps it's troubling to you as well. And so I offer this book as a kind of counterpoint to that type of thinking—as a compelling reminder that *most* of our faith-based organizations stand on the side of good, and that *most* of us need the kind of moral compass only our churches and synagogues and mosques can provide.

One of the great takeaways for me as I talked to people while researching this book was that it's not enough to simply give voice to the idea that we must each do our part, or even to shine a light on the meaningful ways the folks you've met in these pages are making a difference in their communities. No, we need to do better than to just champion these champions. We need to do more. We need to stand in that light ourselves and find a way to be a light for others.

Another great takeaway: Faith cuts both ways. Yes, it's on each of us to define how that faith might look and what it might mean, but at the same time it's also on our religious institutions to have a little faith in its members. Lisa Liberatore, the woman on Long Island who developed that network of assisted-living homes for young adults like her son on the autism spectrum, offers a terrific example of this, when she shares that leadership at the Greek Orthodox church she and her husband belong to so readily agreed to support her in her mission—*before* it was even clear to them what that support might entail.

They were saying yes to Lisa and her family, so let us remember that it falls to each of us, from time to time, to say yes to each other.

And a final takeaway: We need to understand, as the Pittsburgh archivist Eric Lidji has come to understand, all the ways we might open our hearts.

Some readers might recall the title of my last book: *It's Up to Us: Ten Little Ways We Can Bring About Big Change.* I wrote it because when I was running for president in 2016, people kept asking me what was wrong in this country and how to stand in the face of so much polarization and hatred. They'd say, "What are you going to do about it, Governor?" And I'd just put the question back on them and ask, "What are *you* going to do about it?"

Still, I thought I owed people an answer, and the book was

meant to outline some of the things we could *all* do to set things right.

I went back and forth with the publisher over that title, by the way. I thought for a while there should be an exclamation point—*It's Up to Us!* You know, to really stress the clarion call I hoped the book might sound.

Alas, I lost that battle with the publisher, but I'm still sounding the call. In many ways, this book is that exclamation point, so let me repeat myself.

It's up to us!

It's up to us, each of us, to be the change we want to see in this world!

It's up to us, each of us, to tap our religious institutions and faith-based communities to help us redouble our efforts and make a difference!

It's up to us, each of us, to be a source of hope for others, a source of calm for others, and a source of strength for others!

It would be easy to dismiss these words as platitudes or bromides, but I offer them here in full voice and with all sincerity. That exclamation point, for me, is faith, and here I want to go that earlier definition one better: On a more spiritual level, faith is believing in something bigger than ourselves and trusting that there is a higher power to guide us on this earthly plane and lead us to a bright eternity. Now, I understand that this is where a lot of folks throw up their hands and give up on religion, because they have a hard time believing in something so elusive, so intangible. But when you consider what the people you've met in these pages have done in their communities, it doesn't leave room for a whole lot of skepticism. They couldn't necessarily see the outcomes of whatever mission or initiative or *thing* they set out to accomplish, but they knew with certainty that a measure of good would come on the back of their efforts, and that those efforts needed doing. This, of course, is faith as well.

With each of the stories I've shared, you'll find an individual or a group of individuals working within an existing framework with an institution they trusted to provide them with moral support and a variety of resources. They came to count on those resources—funding, staffing, outreach, infrastructure—as they set off to be of service to others. And that's a beautiful thing, right? They could look on and think of that support as a ratification of the righteousness of their cause, and at the same time an *elevation* of that cause, and as we consider these stories in full, it is my great hope that those who are judgmental about religion or those who have dismissed the idea of observing in an organized way might discover a new pathway to follow. They might read these stories and think, *Gee, I never knew these institutions got involved in their communities in this way.* Or, *It never occurred to me to look to my church as a place for civic engagement.* At a time when our country is so divided, I'm hoping people can take a look at this book and change the ways they think about organized religion, and that maybe the examples of these good people will help to dial down the anger and mistrust so many people seem to be feeling. I'm hoping this book can jump-start a new and important conversation about the many ways we might lift each other up instead of all the ways we seem to be dragging each other down.

Let's stop second-guessing each other on what we choose to believe and how we choose to practice our beliefs and focus instead on caring for each other. I think we would all do well to heed the words of Christa Carrero, the woman we met who runs that wonderful therapeutic farm in Hamilton, Ohio. "Our animals don't judge," she reminds us. "All they know is to be loving and supportive and compassionate."

Look, if we care for one another, if we love one another, if we look to live a life bigger than ourselves, there's a way to do that through our institutions of faith, and if it works out that we have an idea for how to make the world a better place, there's a way to put that idea into practice through these institutions as well.

Robert Putnam, the noted political scientist, talks about the *we* in American life, as opposed to the *I*, and I believe you can find that same ethic at play in these pages. These stories might inspire us to restore a sense of togetherness to our communities and look inside ourselves to become a part of that effort. I'm reminded of that line you often hear from actors telling us there are no small parts in a play. The same holds true of the good works you might do. There are no small contributions you might make; there is only recognizing a problem or a failure or a shortcoming of some kind and making an effort to address it in what ways you can.

Remember the world-class theologians I wrote about in the opening to this book? I want to circle back to that effort and share another passage John Palafoutas and I wrote in hopes of getting this group of deep thinkers to speak with one voice into our ever-evolving conversation about God and religion at a time when the church was under fire for not pushing politics.

"We all agree that religion and faith have been eroded in our society," we offered at the time, in an attempt to move that conversation along. "The depths of that erosion can certainly be discussed, but we believe that organized religion is not providing the leadership and moral orientation it once provided for a great many Americans. Why? Well, religious organizations have too often digressed into the political world in an alarming way and are no longer helping educate our citizenry in how to live together with differences. The polarization marked by the talk shows and issue-driven programming involves too much politics, too much judgment, and too much of the animosity that alienates Americans from the common purposes that lie at the heart of our republic. For a variety of reasons, organized religion is struggling to provide access to ultimate centers of value anchored in God."

Not bad, huh? But, as I shared earlier, our efforts didn't really move the needle with this group of theologians, so we moved on. An evolution in my thinking on this issue eventually led me to want to shine a light on the good people and religious communities I've introduced you to here.

So what does it all mean?

Well, I'm not here to tell you what to believe or how to believe. That's personal. We observe and pray in our own ways—or not at all. But what I've learned from these accounts is that we don't go it alone. That there is strength and uplift in numbers. That the collective power of our mosques, synagogues, churches, and other religious organizations can help us to achieve our loftiest goals.

The threads that run through these stories are an indomitable spirit, a never-say-die attitude, and a fierce determination to overcome all obstacles. In every case, the selfless individuals profiled here have met their selfless goals with the help of our religious institutions, which provided the bulwark of their support—financially, materially, spiritually.

My hope is that, taken together, their stories might help us find our own ways forward, to stand as a kind of beacon, and to remind us that there are many reasons to be optimistic about where we're heading in this country. Consider the pattern of forgiveness from the people in Charleston who suffered an unmentionable tragedy and the pastor who was called to lead that community on a path to healing; the call to remember embodied in the work of the archives that came together almost organically in response to the horrifying synagogue shooting in Pittsburgh; the miraculous extra efforts of a man who met Mother Teresa and was inspired to feed more than half a million people every single day; the filmmaker in Portland who helped to transform his own neighborhood school, and then hundreds of schools across the country, through a network of school-church partnerships that helped to elevate our communities and remind our young people that they matter; the sister in New York who helped to create a safe haven for victims of human trafficking; the pastor in the Los Angeles projects who found it in his heart, and in his congregation, to help former gang members and ex-convicts in his community to create lives out of no life at all. Consider all of these strong-willed and passionate people and the religious institutions they were able to call on for support and imagine what *you* can accomplish and the good works *you* can help to bring about with the help of like-minded souls in your own communities.

And don't stop there.

Consider these things, and imagine these things, and then go out and do something about them. Attach them to your own life and circumstances in ways that might matter to you, to your family, to your friends and neighbors.

Make a difference, for, as it says in Proverbs 22:9, "the generous will themselves be blessed."

I'm reminded as well of the parable of the good Samaritan. Most of us know this story, which tells of a man on his way from Jerusalem to Jericho who was attacked and beaten and stripped of his worldly possessions and left for dead by the side of the road. Soon after, a priest came along and noticed the man, but he stepped past him, continuing on his own journey. Then another man passed, and he, too, ignored the suffering traveler. Finally, the good Samaritan happened by and took pity on this broken, beaten man. He went to him and bandaged his wounds, and then he placed him on his donkey and walked with him to the nearest inn, where he gave the innkeeper some coins and asked him to look after the ailing man.

The good Samaritan said, "I will pass this way on my return, and I will reimburse you for any expense you might have."

The great lesson here, to me, has always been that we cannot count on our religious leaders to right *all* the wrongs they see in our society, just as we cannot count on our common brethren to step from their paths and do what's so transparently right. In the end, we can ask only ourselves to meet these moments, at the crossroads of faith and personal responsibility.

One of the questions I'm asked most often is how we might turn things around in this country. Well, it doesn't start with someone else. It starts with you and me and the resources that lie in wait when we look to a higher power. It starts with us. With an exclamation point! And so the next time you drive past a church or a synagogue or a mosque, don't roll your eyes or think negatively about the role religion may or may not play in your life going forward.

Think instead of the very many ways our faith-based communities can and do lift us onto a higher plane.

Think of the exponential power to be found when we walk common ground with our brothers and sisters and reach out our hands, together, to bring others along with us.

Think of the spiritual inspiration that lies in wait, ready to be of service, as we seek to repair the world.

Think of what it means, and what it might take, for you to be a good shepherd in your life—knowing full well that when you have good shepherds, the flock does well. Knowing, too, that the people I've introduced you to in this book are all good shepherds and that it is within each and every one of us to be a good shepherd to those around us.

And, at last, think of the power to be found in starting small. It can be an intimidating thing to look at the great organization someone like Hal Donaldson has built with Convoy of Hope, feeding more than half a million people each day. How can any one of us set out to make such a meaningful difference? Or how about the impossible dream visited on that former synagogue president Bob Freeman, who had this beautiful vision of building an interfaith community where members of his temple could worship alongside members of a local mosque and a local church? How do you navigate and negotiate your way to *that* kind of hopeful outcome?

Well, one way to do that is to think within reach. That's the galvanizing power in the lesson we've just learned from Jillana

Gobel—the woman in Oregon who made it her mission to transform the foster care system in her home state, and eventually across the country, who reminds us that the key to success is not getting out there and trying to do too much all at once but in endeavoring to do just a little bit more each time out, and a little bit more after that, and on and on.

And think of the shining example of Albert Lexie, the unassuming shoeshine man I wrote about in the opening pages—the one who featured so prominently in my first book. A man who was able to donate more than $200,000 to a local children's hospital, all generated from tip money he'd earned while shining shoes at $3 a pop. Talk about small steps!

Just think of it.

ACKNOWLEDGMENTS

It takes many hands to write a book—at least, for *me*, it has always been a team effort, and I could never have written this book without the support of a great many people. I want to thank Beth Hansen, Trevor Johnson, Jim Lynch, and Chevy Hinderlong, who work with me on a daily basis, for helping me to organize my schedule and think through the themes and lessons to be found in the stories I've shared here.

Thanks as well to Rich Nathan, Scott Jenkins, Stephen Steinour, Lori Cohen, Bob Walter, Moshe Banin, Brian Tringali, Bobby Shriver, and Susie Buffett for introducing me to many of the people we ended up interviewing for the book, and to our wonderful team at Zondervan, led by Webster Younce and Paul Pastor, who have faithfully shepherded this book through publication and onto bookstore shelves across the country.

I also want to thank Tremper Longman, the theologian and scholar, who's given me so much good insight into the workings of fate.

I am especially grateful to my longtime friend John Palafoutas, who has been a wonderful source of strength and guidance over the years, and who encouraged me early on in this effort and joined me in thinking there was an important message to be shared on the power of faith to bring our dreams within reach. And to my wife,

Karen Kasich, my first and best reader, for weighing in with note and comment and lending a fresh perspective to the material.

Since leaving the governor's mansion in 2019, I have relied on my agents at United Talent Agency for the public-facing aspects of my post-political career, particularly my good friends David Buchalter and Jennifer Rohrer, who get a nod for setting this project in motion. And Dan Milaschewski, in UTA's literary department, was instrumental in finding the perfect home for this project at Zondervan, so he gets a nod as well.

I am also indebted to my former literary agents, Jenny Bent and John Silbersack, for establishing me as a bestselling author with my previous books, and for introducing me to my longtime collaborator Daniel Paisner. This is the fifth book Dan and I have worked on together. Three of them were *New York Times* bestsellers. Our most recent book, *It's Up to Us*, didn't make the list, but in many ways it stands as the progenitor for this one, sounding a call to readers to be the change they want to see in their communities.

For this book, Dan and I changed things up a bit. In the past, Dan and I would sit together and talk through the stories of my life and career or work our way through material I might write on my own. This time around, it fell to Dan to line up the interviews and research the individuals and organizations we meant to highlight, and to do whatever he could to help me tell these stories—more of a true *collaboration* than the other books we worked on together. The result, I believe, is a book that can truly change the ways we think about faith and altruism, and hopefully inspire readers to think of ways they might tap their own faith communities to make a meaningful difference in their parts of the world.

Finally, I want to acknowledge the bighearted individuals who so graciously shared their stories with us. I want to thank them for the good works they're doing and for recognizing the value in inviting me into their worlds to write about it.